Dr. Alaska

Dr. Alaska

Yukon Valley, Alaska Hospital Novel

Jillian David

TULE
PUBLISHING

Dedication

For those family, friends, and colleagues who recently learned that I write books and are picking up *this* book as the first one to read, listen to me carefully. If you think you see something familiar about this story, you do not. It is fiction, people!

This book is also dedicated to my amazing rural locums FP/Ob colleague, Liz, from Alaska. I really did ask you all of those questions out of fascination and curiosity. It just so happened that your answers got incorporated into a book.

Chapter One

MONDAY MIDMORNING AND Dr. Lee Tipton knew she'd been bitten by the bad-decision bug when she walked to her rental car and her nostrils immediately froze on the first inhalation of crisp Fairbanks, Alaska, air. In early January, no less.

Crisp air? More like *shatteringly frigid air*.

File this last-minute family-medicine-locums assignment under *seemed like a good decision at the time*. She patted her leather purse. Thank God the job would be lucrative. The only thing keeping her credit card functional was a generous credit limit, which was good news and extremely bad news.

Criminelly, Lee hadn't felt her toes for at least a hundred miles as she steered the sedan west along a two-lane state highway that paralleled the Tanana River, soon to join up with the Yukon River. Not that her view would change—all rivers were frozen solid this time of year.

The relentless *thuddidda-thuddidda* rumble of studded tires on glazed, uneven asphalt rocked her into a mind-numbing haze. Low clouds blended with the snow-covered pine trees, barren hills, and mountains, visible out the fogged windshield in an unending white and gray scene of hypothermia. Every so often, there was a break in the terrain revealing two tracks that led off into the hills or stopped at an isolated house. The only humans who survived out here had to be rugged, resourceful, and unable to quit.

So, the exact opposite type of person as Lee.

Good life choices? *Ha.* Lee let out a hollow laugh in the car. No way. This assignment served as an escape, pure and simple. She had gone as far as possible from everything back home. This job would also be the ladder for her to climb out of the financial hole she'd fallen into. Why else would she ever travel to Alaska's interior in January?

She rolled her achingly cold fingers in the Thinsulate gloves she'd found at an outdoor store before she'd left Georgia. Apparently, when the product advertised TEN BELOW, that number didn't indicate comfort, just survival.

A gust of wind buffeted the rental sedan. The subzero chill permeating the vehicle fought against the meager warmth from the heater vents. At least she had some comfort. She shifted her butt on the warm seat—oh yes, she'd set the tush-warmer to *inferno*, second-degree gluteal burns be damned.

What she'd give for a hot and steamy ninety degrees in Alpharetta, Georgia, land of sundresses, sandals, mimosa brunches, and the glow of perma-sweat.

Instead, she had perma-freeze.

Lordie knew her socialite mother would curl up like a frozen doodlebug if she could see Lee now, shivering in her thick gloves, shapeless puffy coat, and static-y hair shoved under a yarn cap.

Mom. Bless her heart, but her image-preoccupied society

parent was focused on what damage Lee's divorce might do to *Mom's* well-being and the damage a divorce would do to a family that kept up appearances at all costs. That one fact played a big part in why Lee was currently driving this tin can over swirling snow. Still, Lee wanted even more distance between herself and her bad decisions. She stared out the window and blinked in the bright yet low light.

In her rearview mirror, a truck that had been creeping up to her for miles finally pulled around and sped away, with a diesel growl and puffs of fading exhaust, replaced once more by wind and mind-numbing studded tire road noise. Lee shook her head as red taillights disappeared in the distance. The posted speed limit didn't exist as a challenge on a wintry day like this. Common sense still counted for something.

She squinted ahead, expecting to see the outskirts of the town. Not much else other than frozen tundra.

What a place to run away from that money-sucker her parents had pushed her into marrying. Worst of all? She had found out that Preston Dupree IV had not only used her family connections to get a seat on the Alpharetta City Council, but he'd had an affair while Lee was in her early years of practice in Dahlonega. Then, he had drained her hard-earned savings account drier than Lake Lanier in a drought. His need to project success required a big house and bigger toys and exclusive golf memberships and vacations in places with expensive hotels.

Mom and Dad had approved of the show of wealth. Of course they did. Lord forbid, they should ever decline hosting a cocktail party to support the local political campaign *du jour*.

The whole time, Lee had been too buried in three years of family medicine residency, then the rural obstetrics fellowship for a year, then practice. She hadn't seen what occurred right under her nose. At least not until last fall when, at the age of thirty-five, Lee's carefully planned world crumbled under her. All the while, her parents were more worried about the financial and social impact of Lee's divorce on *them*.

She rubbed her eyes. Hard to believe her parents had encouraged her to stick with Preston. Heck, after the divorce went through, he had even tried to raise funds by filing a HIPAA suit with her employer. He falsely alleged that Lee had discovered the affair by going into the chart of a patient—his girlfriend—whom she didn't treat. The only time Lee was thankful for an electronic medical record that tracked every log-in and click was when she sat in the office of the hospital's human resources department to defend herself.

Bull crap and good riddance to him. *Fool me once*, as the saying went. When Lee trusted any man again, it'd be a cold day in hell.

Welp. She peered out the frosted window, careful what she wished for.

Brake lights glowed red and grew larger. She took her foot off the pedal. All Lee knew about traveling during Georgia ice storms was to stay home. That and, if you had to drive, maneuver like Granny was sitting in the passenger seat, wearing her best Sunday dress while holding an open container of church potluck gravy on her lap. Lee let the speed drop and gripped the wheel, easing over to what she hoped was the road shoulder.

Four wheels of the upside-down truck spun slowly, the cab resting at the bottom of a short embankment. Her heart pounded. Someone was in there, possibly hurt. She stopped the car, zipped up the neck of her puffy Columbia jacket, and secured the gloves. One step out of the car, and she bit back a curse as the wind cut plumb through her twill pants.

But Lee was a doctor. Ignoring an accident with no one else around? Not an option. A burst of adrenaline along with the ABCDEs of trauma assessment flashed through her mind.

Distant sirens echoed eerily over the otherwise empty landscape. Faint flashes of red lights penetrated the blowing snow.

A weak groan coming from inside the vehicle got her attention. No time to wait for EMS. She gritted her teeth and scooched down the few feet of snowy embankment to the forty-five-degree upended cab. The front grille had quite a dent in it.

Her ankles chilled as snow worked under her pant legs.

Reaching the driver's-side door, she peeked down into the busted window and gasped when a bloody hand waved, next to an upside-down face.

Adrenaline giving her extra strength, she pulled on the inverted door. A man, looking to be in his late sixties, reached toward her, and she yelped. "Hold on, sir. Don't move. Let's get you stabilized."

Spine precautions, airway evaluation, cardiac assessment. Could she do anything to help? Sirens blared, closer now.

"Oh hell, I'm fine. I already called 911 right when I realized I wasn't going anywhere without a tow. State trooper will be here in a while," he groused, his lips moving within a dense salt-and-pepper beard. "Damn moose. Should've known. I was due. It's been a few years since my last head-on." Blood flowed upward from a gash at his temple, due to gravity, turning his gray hair red.

To Lee's shock, the man unbuckled, gripped the truck frame, and heaved himself out, his leather and shearling coat scraping as he exited. She held the door and tried to steady him as he sat down at the bottom of the bank with a guttural *oof*. At least he moved all extremities well. For now.

She pressed a gloved hand against the briskly bleeding injury that now ran down his face instead of up it. She tried to get him to lie down, but he waved her off until she insisted.

"Fine. For you, I'll cooperate," he grumped, reclining against the bank in his coat and thick snow pants.

"Don't move. You could have other serious injuries." With her other gloved hand, she pressed against the opposite side of his neck, creating makeshift in-line c-spine stabilization between her two hands.

The loud sirens abruptly shut off. Her ears rang in the sudden silence.

"More serious than a broken truck?" He motioned toward the steam still coming from the vehicle. "Damn near going to take forever and a fortune to get it fixed." He grimaced, lines deepening on his leathery face, redirecting rivulets of blood now through the creases. "Who are you?" He squinted one eye as he scanned her. "Some fancy-pants state employee? I passed you a while back, driving like an old person."

"Which one of us in the ditch, sir?"

He grunted but shot her a glare crinkled with laughter.

She made a noncommittal sound and continued her assessment. The guy talked, so he could breathe. Airway was grossly patent. No visible neck bruises or swelling. She considered other possibilities—spine damage, organ contusions, brain injury. He answered her questions with fluid speech. At least cognition remained intact.

"And I'm not government. I'm the temp—"

Two vehicle doors slammed a few feet above her. "All right. We'll take it from here, ma'am." A low, authoritative voice cut through the cold air.

No way was she removing pressure from the bleeding areas. Sure as heck wasn't releasing control of his cervical spine until it was safe to do so. "No, I don't mind helping. I can—"

The man descended the bank, stomping the heels of his thick boots into the ground to create makeshift stairs.

He gave her a curt lift of his chin. "It's nice of you to stop, but let the trained professionals handle it, okay?"

She squinted at the man with light brown hair peeking out from under a navy Yukon Valley EMS beanie, official-looking matching cargo pants with pockets bulging with what she presumed was medical gear, a large square bag slung over one broad shoulder clad in a neon yellow high-visibility jacket. He finished off the look with a patronizing smile and nod.

"Hey," she said, "I'm trying to stabilize his spine and limit his movement, but he isn't cooperative."

He paused. "Like you've seen on medical shows?"

What? Despite the cold, a hot flush sped through her.

She searched for a name on the front of his jacket. STEEN. "You're kidding, right?"

The EMT paused, brown eyebrows drawn together.

Then he shrugged and turned to the patient. "Bruce, you been drinking?"

No way did she wish to be the focus of this rescue, but this guy discounting her response to the scene? The brush-off stuck in her craw. At the end of the day, she didn't care about her pride, though. This patient needed appropriate care.

"Naw," the driver—Bruce—said. "Though I wouldn't mind some hooch right about now." He shifted, and Lee moved her gloved pressure on his wound with him, limiting his range of motion. "This mess"—he waved at the steaming vehicle—"is truck versus moose." He groaned. "Aggie is going to kill me."

"She'll be thankful that moose didn't decapitate you. Then she'll read you the riot act." The EMT glanced at his partner, who had slid down the bank to join them, and they both chuckled.

First of all, who in the world chuckled at a time like this? This guy could have died.

Second of all, Lee was happy to turn over her Good Samaritan duties to the ambulance crew, but would it kill them to give her a tiny bit of credit for initiating the man's care?

Third of all, could a moose really decapitate someone?

The EMT winked a startling blue eye at her. Up close, she spied a few fine lines on his face, suggesting he was in his thirties, not twenties as his nimble movements and broad frame implied.

He smiled. "You're not really dressed for the elements, are you?"

Right then, a gust of wind-driven snow barreled right over them, chilling her to the marrow of her bones. Her toes curled in the snow melting inside her Gianni Bini leather booties. She had thought this choice of footwear would be professional, stylish, yet rugged.

Instead, they were damp and cold. And probably ruined.

"Come on, Bruce, let's check you over," Steen, the medic, said.

"I'm just a little banged up. No need to go to any trouble. I can walk back to town or wait for a trooper to give me a lift," he grumbled.

The EMT shook his head. "No can do, Bruce. Aggie would feed us to the brown bears if we didn't do our job." He motioned to his partner, a younger woman with dark hair in a ponytail that trailed from under a leather hat that had two fur-lined flaps pulled down over her ears. "Louise, let's get him on the board."

Lee maintained c-spine control while the two EMTs log-rolled and then secured Bruce onto the backboard. Only after they fastened the cervical collar and velcroed the orange foam blocks in place did Lee release in-line stabilization. Steen taped a thick gauze bandage on the bleeding head wound and secured it with Coban wrap, giving Bruce an old-school sweatband appearance. A quick pulse-ox check showed a heart rate of eighty-five and oxygen saturation of ninety-eight percent.

Bruce continued to answer questions. Heck, he continued to tell stories nonstop while the medics worked. He was cognitively intact. She sighed. Thank goodness.

The medics efficiently snugged all the straps on the board, then Lee grabbed an open handle slot near his knees and helped the medics lift the patient.

She wiggled her fingers in the cooling dampness and shivered. Her glove was likely ruined. What a great first day at her new job.

Bruce kept griping as they eased him, firmly secured, up the few feet of the bank. Lee pushed the end of the backboard as the medics pulled.

After the EMTs lifted the backboard onto the gurney, Steen turned back to her. Lee had little to no traction with the booties and was stuck at the bottom of the bank.

"Want help?" He knelt, took off his thick glove, and reached down.

Removing the glove that wasn't saturated, she took the EMT's offered outstretched hand—not EMT, paramedic. She'd read the lettering on the back of his coat when he set his bag down and turned. His grip was strong and steady as he easily pulled her up the last few slippery feet onto the highway shoulder. The sudden bout of breathlessness had to be due to the steep scramble.

He tightened his hand around hers. "Hey, thank you again for stopping. Not all citizens would have done that."

"I'm not just a—" She took a deep breath, which unfortunately caused crystals to form in her nostrils, and she coughed for ten seconds. Finally, she managed to wave her free arm at him. "Sure. Glad to help." The man continued to hold her hand, his other hand resting on her shoulder, steadying her. Those two pressure points were the only warm areas on her body right now.

"Uh, need help getting anywhere?" Paramedic Steen asked, a friendly glint in his glacier-lake blue eyes.

"Nope, just going to Yukon Valley."

He frowned, then stepped away and pulled on his glove. "Up the road a few miles. Thataway."

Then he pointed. Actually pointed. As if there were any other destinations on the only two-lane road in the middle of absolutely nowhere, which went to one place. Yukon Valley. Lee giggled.

A full-body icy shiver sobered her up in a hurry. Wow, she'd never experienced cold like this. She shoved her bare hand back in her glove and stared at his broad upper torso, which was where her eye level rested. How toasty it would be if Paramedic Steen were to unzip that safety jacket and tuck her against his chest. She swallowed. Talk about an inappropriate thought.

Besides, the guy had underestimated her.

Lee hated being underestimated.

The other medic prepared to load Bruce into the rig. Bruce winced as Louise peeked under the wrapped gauze on his forehead. Trussed with safety straps on the backboard, he had nowhere to go.

He blew a raspberry. "You're not getting a five-star rating on bedside manner, Louise."

"Tough." She fake-swatted at him. "A minute ago, you were planning to walk home. Let me work, or I'm telling Aggie that you're a terrible patient and you don't listen."

Bruce went stock-still.

Paramedic Steen pointed a thumb up and behind him, drawing Lee's gaze from his chest to his sheepish grin. "So, I should …"

"Yes. Patient." Her teeth started to chatter. Lee waved with her blood-soaked glove toward Bruce as she fished out her car keys from the coat pocket with her other hand. "Good luck to you, sir."

Bruce wiggled a few unrestrained fingers in her direction. "I'll be fine. No thanks to this guy. Look at him. He's more interested in making goo-goo eyes at you than taking care of his mortally injured patient!" He hollered, "I'm suffering here, people!"

Chapter Two

*H*E'S MORE INTERESTED *in making goo-goo eyes at you than his mortally injured patient.*

Whoa. Those were fighting words if Maverick Steen had ever heard them. No way would he shirk his paramedic duties to moon over some onlooker. Also, he never made *goo-goo eyes*. Ever. Not anymore.

Enter Bruce, the town troublemaker, pot-stirring again.

Not that Bruce was completely wrong. The bystander *was* interesting. Even with those ridiculous leather shoes, the young woman came only to his chin. He studied her. Only, she wasn't exactly young. In her thirties? Hard to tell. Her light brown eyes flashed wide, and little puffs of vapor came from red lips. Snow clung to and melted on the damp bottoms of what were definitely *not* winter pants. Tiny flakes of snow skidded across her bright blue, brand-spanking-new name-brand puffy jacket. He snorted. Those coats might advertise that they could keep people warm so many degrees below zero, but Mav knew better. No way did she have proper layering of any kind. Hell, she was dressed like she was headed to a business meeting.

What business was out here, this far from Fairbanks, near the literal end of the road? Maybe she was lost.

"Are you okay?" he asked as she shivered. For a split second, he wanted to pull her to him, wrap his arms around her, and warm her up.

"Shouldn't you be attending our patient?" Her mellow voice had a lilt, and he struggled to place the accent.

Then again, she could figure out how to warm herself up.

He rocked back on his heels. "*Our* patient?" He rubbed his chin with a gloved hand.

Huh. He pushed his shoulders back and puffed his chest out. He and Louise made a good EMS team, efficient and skilled.

With a wise nod, he said, "Well, quality care *is* everyone's job."

The woman rolled her eyes and snorted.

He stared down at her, momentarily speechless. That was one of his best bullshit healthcare team lines.

Never let it be said that Maverick Steen couldn't recover in the face of adversity. "You'll get hypothermia if you stay out here much longer." See? Hard to argue with good, solid logic. "We're trying to limit the number of patients out here," he quipped, briefly resting his hand on her upper arm. There was something about the woman that made him want to maintain contact.

With a grunt that managed to sound both sexy and judgmental, she planted her mittened fists on her hips. "*Hmmph.*"

He dropped his hand to his side. "What—"

"Y'all are going to need to get him some CT scans to

check for injuries." *Y'all*. Southern, then. Alabama? Having lived in Alaska his entire life, he was no expert in lower forty-eight dialects. Mav had, however, been forced by his mother to watch *Steel Magnolias* years ago, and the woman in front of him kind of sounded like the characters.

Fine, he'd seen the movie twice.

Okay, three times. But only because of the film's portrayal of a character who had type one diabetes, which held medical interest to him. No other reason to rewatch it, such as a riveting storyline or excellent acting.

Damn it. He hadn't said anything for several seconds. He needed to ask her a question so she'd talk again. Maybe she would say more about how she came to be at the accident. People got excited when they helped out EMS.

Oftentimes, bystanders thought that working accidents was like one of those medical TV shows. However, her actions showed that this woman had some sort of medical training. Likely a nurse or medical assistant.

He gravely dipped his head. "Don't worry. We'll get him over to the hospital and let the doctors to do a full checkup."

He didn't miss how she stiffened.

Bruce piped up. "No, we will not!"

Louise hissed, "Do you want me to call your wife? Because I will do it. Aggie's number is in my contacts."

"Ah, geez, Louise, you have to hit me where it hurts."

"She's right, Bruce," Mav said. "We'll never hear the end of it from Aggie if we don't get you proper care. She's got rheumatoid arthritis and is already tired. Do you want to stress her out any more?"

Louise glared at Bruce.

Bruce glared over at Mav.

The city-slicker woman continued to glare at Mav.

Oh, come on. Two against one.

The golden glow of the woman's skin had become snow-drift pale, and the fancy ripstop nylon coat fabric *shushed* as shivers made her small frame shake. Another burst of need to warm her up and be the reason she stopped shivering hit him like an avalanche. His hand halfway reached her before he stopped the instinctive impulse.

"Hmm. I can see my work here is done." Her teeth might be chattering, but she still rolled her pretty brown eyes at him.

Pretty?

A flash hit him. He needed to know how long she would be in the area, what the hell she was doing out here, what her plans were for dinner. How bad of a conflict of interest was it to ask for her number while on a call in the field, neglecting his actual patient?

First of all, Bruce was medically stable.

Mav immediately stomped all of those lines of thought. He was the town's EMS chief. He had to set an example. Second of all, Mav had one dating rule, and he had almost broken it right here. No *cheechakos*, as the villagers liked to disparagingly call them. Outsiders. Besides, Mav knew better, even if the ratio of eligible women in Yukon Valley wasn't in his favor. He'd learned his lesson a few years ago. This frozen princess was no different.

His mind stopped churning long enough for him to say,

"Hey, why don't you go get warmed up?" See? Helpful. Not pushy. Considerate.

Dumb! his inner voice chided him.

"I've got it. Will do." She peered around him one more time. "Take care, Bruce."

"Thanks, dear." He barked toward the open rig door, "Hey, Louise, I'm freezing my venison off here. Get me in that nice warm ambulance already!"

Louise shook her head, held her palms up to the sky, and mouthed *Why me?*

The blue lights of a state trooper vehicle grew brighter. Mav had known the trooper would take a while, being that Lieutenant Kate was the only one in this area and had been ten miles to the west of town when dispatch sent him and Louise out on the call. Dumb luck that they had just finished a transport from the hospital to a patient's home in this general vicinity.

Suddenly, Mav didn't know what to do with his hands as he stared at the woman. "Um, enjoy your visit to the area." He tried to shove them in pockets but missed.

"Visit. Sure thing. Y'all take care." She hurried to the sedan and opened the door on the second try. He could see her through the partially fogged front windshield.

Kate pulled up in the Alaska State Trooper vehicle with its typical matte black roof and rolled down her window.

Louise called out, "You going to do any work today, Mav, or keep staring at the nice lady?"

He hurried over and helped slide the gurney into the back of the rig to prove he was focused on his job. "Let me give Kate a quick update." He stopped at the trooper's car for a minute. The trooper took notes, then strolled to the citizen's car for a statement. Their voices drifted over to him.

Mav closed the back doors of the ambulance and chanced one more glance at the woman. Her golden hair glinted even in the dimming late-afternoon light as she talked with Lieutenant Kate. Shaking his head, he walked to the front of the vehicle, got in the front seat, and drove away.

He'd missed an opportunity.

And dodged a proverbial bullet.

Chapter Three

T HERE WAS COLD—AND then there was melted-snow-in-thin-leather-booties cold. Hells bells, Lee would never get warm again. She checked the car's GPS—another four miles to Yukon Valley. The bottled water and disinfecting gel had dried the heck out of her hands, but at least she'd removed the blood that had seeped through her glove.

As she approached town, more snow-covered roads exiting the highway began to appear, along with a smattering of homes and mailboxes. The evidence of civilization after driving for several hours through Arctic tundra released the tight muscles around her neck and shoulders. Five minutes later, she spied a YUKON VALLEY WARMLY WELCOMES YOU sign. Lee snickered as she peered through the windshield at snowy, bare hills on one side of town and mountains rising up from the other side of what might be the ice-covered Yukon River.

She squinted at small figures on the ice. Oh gosh, were there people on snowmobiles out there? Lordie, was it safe? Must be. They took sled dogs on frozen rivers, right? Snowmobiles weren't much different. She imagined ice cracking beneath her feet if she were to stand out there.

She drove slowly, head on a swivel. Where was the actual

town?

A broad one-story log-cabin-style building appeared. Next to it, neon fuel prices glowed brightly on a marquee above the pumps. Three vehicles idled outside the store, constant puffs of exhaust vapor emitting from the tailpipes. Red lettering on white background above the store's main entrance read THREE BEARS ALASKA, and to the side of the door were several smaller signs identifying grocery, pharmacy, delicatessen, bait and tackle, automotive, office supplies, and sporting goods. Welp. All bases covered.

Lee shivered. She should stop back later for better winter gear.

Another half mile farther, Lee turned right at the ice-flocked, battered blue H sign, traveling a residential block off the highway to reach Yukon Valley Hospital. Putting the car into park on the snow-covered gravel lot, where the front row of spaces each contained a strange white box on a three-foot pole, she studied the scene in front of her. She wasn't sure what she had expected, but this modest compact building with river stone entryway surrounded by ten-foot-high mounds of snow wasn't it. On the end of the building was another sliding door with a bright red emergency sign lit overhead. This facility was nothing like the high-rise Atlanta hospitals or even the roomy hospital campus in Dahlonega where she'd practiced before.

Before her life and career had imploded.

She hurried toward the hospital, pulling up the hood of her coat. No bloody gloves—talk about a bad impression. Instead, she shoved her hands into her pockets as her boots squeaked on a few inches of fluffy snow that hadn't yet been plowed.

The slate blue and earth tones of the interior and gust of warm air welcomed her right along with the balding middle-aged man at the front desk.

"Can I help you?" he said with a smile.

"Dr. Tipton here to meet … um …" Dang it, she had left her printed itinerary in the car. She glanced over her shoulder, dreading another walk outside.

"Deirdre, the chief nursing officer."

"Yes! How—"

"Psychic!" Another grin as he punched in a number on the phone. "We don't get many new faces here, and she let me know our new doctor was coming in for orientation."

She protested, "I'm only a temporary—"

He lifted his hand in a gentle gesture to wait. "Hi, Deirdre, this is Billy. Dr. Tipton is here." Putting down the phone, he said, "She'll be right out. How was your drive? Do you need anything? Restroom? Water?" He tilted his head, one eyebrow raised, and pulled a face. "Stiff drink?"

A laugh burst from her as she gave him her coat when he offered. "Restroom, thanks." Lee ducked in and cleaned her hands once again. A stiff drink wouldn't hurt. One to shore up her nerves for this massive dive into the unknown. When she was thirteen, she had jumped off a friend's dock on Lake Windward, thinking the warm water was only a few feet deep. Instead, Lee went down, down, down until she finally touched the muddy, debris-strewn bottom of the lake ten feet below. Took an eternity to float back up through the warm greenish haze.

This hospital assignment had a lot of similarities to that no-air, too-deep type of situation. Lee sucked in a big breath, dried her hands, smoothed her work clothes, and pasted on what she hoped was a professional yet pleasant expression.

A woman who appeared around Lee's age with bright blue eyes, a bob of chestnut hair, gray business slacks, and a casual blazer approached from the desk, hand already out. "Hello, Dr. Tipton. Deirdre Steen, so nice to meet you."

Steen? Like the paramedic? What were the chances? "Ah, you, too," Lee stammered, shaking her hand.

"We're so glad you're here." She beamed. "Our two remaining doctors are pretty tired. We were short-staffed before, but now? Phew."

Right, because Lee was covering for the third doctor who was out on maternity leave. "Happy to help."

"Well. Ready for the grand tour?"

"Hope you like it here, Dr. Tipton." Billy waved, then answered the ringing phone, "Yukon Valley Hospital, how can I direct your call?"

Deirdre handed Lee a badge and pager with a sheepish expression. "Cell phones aren't always reliable. Good to have a backup means of communication. Though if you're out in the bush, neither will work. Plan your call days accordingly." She motioned. "Let's start in the ED." They badged through automatic double doors.

The buzz of light bustling activity greeted them.

At the nurses' station, Lee asked, "Is Bruce here?"

The ED nurse frowned at Deirdre.

"I stopped to help him when his truck flipped on the highway," Lee explained.

"Oh, that was *you*?" The nurse's brows rose. "Mav said some *cheechako* was climbing all over Bruce's truck."

Deirdre's head whipped around with a hiss, and the nurse clamped her mouth shut.

"Sorry," the woman said.

Mav? *Chee*-what?

An EMT with familiar broad shoulders who had brown hair peeking out from under his beanie was pulling an empty ambulance gurney out of a trauma bay. "Hi, Dee," he called, glancing back. Then his big smile dropped into a frown as he turned to Lee. "What are you doing here?"

Her cheeks heated. Had all the various monitors stopped beeping in the ED? No one moved.

Deirdre motioned. "Dr. Tipton, Maverick Steen, my little brother and Yukon Valley's head EMT. And sometime troublemaker." She poked him in the ribs, and he yelped, swatting at her.

"We already met over Bruce." Lee chuckled.

Mav opened and closed his mouth. "Doctor?"

Deirdre crossed her arms and pursed her lips. "What? You've never seen one of them, Mav?"

"No. I have. Here. Of course. Lots of other places. It's just … but out there, I didn't—"

Hmm. Someone had gotten too big for his britches.

Lee turned a laugh into a polite cough. "I was incognito, and I didn't give my credentials." Mostly because he didn't let her get a word in edgewise, but whatever. She had way bigger fish to fry today.

"*Oof.* My bad, Doc." He grimaced, somehow making him appear handsome and approachable. "As Sis will tell you, it's par for the course."

"Maverick Steen." Deirdre clapped. "Always tactful and calm under pressure."

"Hey now, Dee. I was only doing my job."

"A simple *nice to meet you, Dr. Tipton* will be the best way out of the hole you've dug."

Lee chuckled as Deirdre skewered her brother with her eyes. *Love to see it.*

He nodded and stuck out his hand with a brief warm press of their palms that made her arm tingle and heart flutter. "Nice to meet you, Doctor. Enjoy the time you have in Yukon Valley."

Lee pulled her chin back. He spoke like she couldn't hack it here. As if he didn't expect her to stick around.

In truth, she had no plans to do so. This temporary job was designed for emotional distance and a financial reset until she could carry on with her life and career.

"Hopefully, I don't see you again," Lee said.

"What?" Mav frowned, brow-furrowed suspicion mixed with hurt puppy.

Almost like he cared what she thought.

Swallowing the foreign sensation of a flutter in her throat, she added, "You know, because I have to cover the ER and hospital? If I don't see you, that means you're not bringing in sick patients for me to work on or transferring critically ill patients to Fairbanks." When he didn't move, she cleared her throat, her mouth suddenly dry. "I'm not above invoking good karma, Murphy's Law, and every other superstition I can think of."

"Uh. Yeah. Me, too, then. Hope not to see you. Around. I guess. Or not. Because of no patients." With a whoosh of air, he turned toward the gurney his EMS partner, Louise, now stood behind with a bemused smile, then looked at the nursing station and then his sister. "Gotta go. Sis. Doc. Geez." He rotated stiffly and pulled the gurney away.

Deirdre made a flourish. "My brother, folks."

The ER nurse smiled. "At least he's cute." She winked at Lee. "And eligible."

Lee's heart rate did a tachycardic flutter then a brady-cardic dip. Tempting, sure. But that particular delicious treat came with two scoops of *nope* with some *when-hell-freezes-over* sprinkles on top. She was still licking her wounds from the divorce. She'd trusted a good-looking guy once. See how that turned out? Clearly, her partner picker was broken.

Even if the awkwardly handsome man in question made her toes tingle.

The toe tingling was probably frostbite.

Deirdre rescued Lee from responding. "Let's head to radiology, med-surg floor, OR, and then to labor and delivery. We'll finish up in the clinic so you can meet everyone there. Dr. Burmeister is seeing that ER patient, so we'll circle back when he's free. Hope you're ready to hit the ground running. Your first twenty-four-hour call starts tomorrow."

Chapter Four

THE FRUSTRATING MONDAY shift finally over, Mav stomped through Three Bears Alaska a little after seven p.m., still gritting his teeth at that bystander not telling him she was a doctor and Deirdre picking on him. He enjoyed living in a small community, most of the time. In Yukon Valley, though, a rumor could make it across town faster than a snowmachine going full throttle on a groomed trail.

He mentally ran his list. Kibble to mix with fish and venison for his ravenous hordes, a new hammer for lodge repairs before the snowmachining guests arrived next month, a pair of wool socks to replace what Kenai had chewed through, and, of course, groceries.

Gotta love Three Bears. They stocked at least one item of everything.

Bonus, the deli was still open. He veered away from his shopping plan to see about thin sliced cold cuts for lunch this week. Mav had canned and dried plenty of salmon and venison for the winter, but he welcomed a change in meat from time to time.

"Hi, Tuli," he said to Tulimak Sampson, a local firefighter and part-time deli employee who Mav had been friends with for years.

"*Gganaa*! What'll it be, Mav?"

"A pound of sliced ham and ten pounds of beef. Can I have some bone-in?"

"For you and the team?"

"Bone broth and treats. Nothing but the best for my babies. The ham's for me."

"Got it." Tuli got to work setting the slicing machine as he weighed and packaged the beef. He said over his shoulder, "Heard you took care of Bruce today."

Mav shifted from foot to foot, warm in his heavy EMS pants, shirt, and jacket. "You know we can't talk about what may or may not have happened at work."

"Aggie dropped by here a few hours ago, so it's not like Bruce's ambulance trip was a secret. Said he was banged up but okay. It sounds like you took over for the new doctor at the wreck." He grinned.

A nasty knot twisted in Mav's gut. Really? That was what people thought? Sheesh. "First of all, if I come upon a wreck and a nonparamedic is there, it's my job to take control of the situation. Hypothetically." He scuffed his salt-rimmed black boot against the blobs of melting snow on the worn linoleum floor. "Just because someone works in healthcare doesn't mean they're experts in prehospital care." He leaned against the counter and pointed a finger. "In fact, more often than not, nonmedics make our jobs harder. You know all about that, working with the fire department and helping on medical calls." The light squeak of grocery carts and low voices in the store behind him created a soothing background.

"Hey, sorry for asking, man!" Tuli piled ham slices on a piece of wax paper on the scale, then packaged up the bundle and handed it and the steak to Mav. "New doctor's cute, yeah?"

Tuli wasn't wrong, damn it. Dr. Tipton's button nose and wind-pinkened cheeks made her brown eyes glow. Hell, in the ED when he'd seen her without the beanie, she took his breath away. The color of those long waves was a rich gold, like aspens in the fall. Off-balance, Mav shook his head. He had to be hypoglycemic.

"How would you know?"

"Bruce raved about her to Aggie, who then told me. Also, Billy's fast on the hospital switchboard."

Mav placed the meat in the cart next to him, keeping his eyes on Tuli. "Why would you, a man too busy to hang out with his friend and watch the Seahawks playoff game last weekend, have time to care what the new doctor looks like?"

"I mean, besides the obvious?" Tuli smirked and motioned in a way that encompassed the sparsely populated town with its lack of relationship prospects, unless cuddling with brown bears counted as companionship.

"Besides, she's been in town for only four hours. How would you know her from anyone? Although I suppose she's easy to pick out, being all city-slicker in fancy clothes and hating the cold, searching for Starbucks and a mall."

Like his ex. Skylar had been a pretty face and nice person who hated every minute out here in Yukon Valley. He had vowed never to make the mistake of investing time in an outsider who didn't love the Alaskan interior like Mav did.

"Because, ah …" Tuli lifted his chin.

Mav's stomach dropped like a rumbling avalanche bore down on him. Slowly, he pivoted. Raised eyebrows above pursed pink lips identified a certain new physician who, yes, looked like she'd prefer a Starbucks and who wore expensive but inadequate gear. She blinked at him. The temperature under his coat shot up twenty degrees.

If Mav was lucky, then she hadn't heard him.

Sweat prickled his lower back. *Say something, damn it.* "Um, getting deli meat?" he managed.

A ghost of a smile came and went. "Is that okay for a city slicker to do here?"

Yep, she'd heard him all right. "Tulimak will fix you right up." He waved toward his useless friend, who had hung Mav out to dry.

Tuli now stood tall with a puffed chest.

"Thanks. Good to know." She curled bare fingers around the cart handle. "Does this store carry any good gloves? I ruined mine while *making your job harder* today."

Geez, exactly how long had she been listening? The pretty doctor must have ears like a bat.

Then, in an unfortunate turn of events, his mouth became uncoupled from good sense. "It's true, you know," he said. "Non-EMS personnel trying to render care in a prehospital setting can be a barrier to doing our job." He barreled ahead like an unpiloted bobsled on a steep track. "Besides, you should have established yourself as a physician back at the accident."

She sucked in a breath, the *whoosh* like an Arctic gale

bearing down on him. "First of all, I didn't see other medical personnel lined up to help at that accident, so it was slim pickings, and we make do with what we've got. Then you cut me off before I could identify myself. However, I'm still confused. Did the capable manner in which I stabilized our patient not make my competence clear?"

That jut of her chin and quirk to her full lips made him want to lean over and soften that mad expression with his mouth.

She continued. "Perhaps in the future I should broadcast proficiency via interpretive dance for all to see."

Then, she smashed his budding fantasy of a commanding kiss by doing a silly arm noodle move combined with the floss dance, finished off with a jazz-hands flourish that turned into two thumbs pointed at her chest. "Ta-da. Helpful medical professional, right here. Better?"

Tuli barked a laugh, and Mav whipped his head around. His so-called friend clamped his mouth shut as he studied the spotless countertop he now carefully wiped. Knowing Tuli, he'd be posting about this encounter online before Mav left the store.

Fine. Mav had made assumptions out in the field, stereotyped, and then pulled rank. All true. But he *was* the Yukon Valley EMS director. That and a dollar would get him a one-dollar cup of coffee. He rubbed his chin.

Time to own up to being human. "Listen, you and I got off on the wrong foot. And the other foot I shoved right into my mouth. Dr. Tipton, I apologize." Eating crow was *not* the activity he wanted to do in front of Tuli.

After a full ten seconds that felt like hours, her shoulders rose and fell, making the puffy coat *shush* in the now-silent deli area. "Okay."

He extended a hand, and she met it with her own icy one. He tamped down a strange need to tug her to him and wrap his arms around her, the second time he'd felt that way today. That sort of move would be about as smart as hugging a grumpy wolverine. He imagined snarls as sharp teeth sank into him. "Good."

"On account of us working together"—she gave a delicate snort—"you should call me Lee." She sighed and gently slid her hand out of his. "So, gloves?"

"Sure. We'll head over to outdoor gear." He took two steps then stopped as Tuli cleared his throat. "Have a good one, man." Knowing his friend, he'd feast on his retellings of Mav and Lee's encounter for weeks.

"Nice to meet you." Lee waggled her fingers.

Tuli waved back, somehow managing to flex his muscled arms. "Welcome to Yukon Valley, *Doctor.*"

Mav shook his head as he led her past produce, cleaning products, ice fishing equipment, and hunting supplies until they reached two small racks of coats and snow pants. On the nearby wall was a display of gloves and mittens.

"Oh, Thinsulate," she said. "That's good, right? My old gloves were this brand."

"It'll work great if the temperature never drops below freezing." He tilted his head as he tried again to place her accent. It wasn't Cajun. "No gloves."

"Really?"

"Unless you need dexterity in the outdoors, it's warmer to go with mittens. How about these Gore-Tex forty-below mittens, paired with glove liners. Or beaver fur mittens have amazing insulative properties."

Her brows drew together as she turned the price tag over. "Maybe not the beaver ones."

"Are you into animal rights?" Another snap judgment. Man, he needed to slow down the pipeline of thoughts-to-mouth.

"No. I mean, yes. Look, I don't love the idea of killing animals for sport, but for food and materials to survive? I understand the circle of life. But the fur-lined cost a lot." She chewed her lower lip. "The Gore-Tex and glove liners are also expensive." Glancing up at him, she shrugged. "Student loans." Her wry smile rocked him back on his heels. "Do I need both types of hand coverings?" she asked.

"If you don't want frostbite after ten minutes when the windchill is below zero, then yes. Get the liner and the impermeable outer mitten." He held up the liner, and she tried it on. Perfect fit. She stood close enough that he caught a whiff of her floral scent. No. Not exactly. He inhaled again. Floral hint mixed with berries. Tart and sweet. Seemed fitting.

She put the items in her cart. "I don't plan on a lot of outdoor activities."

"Not staying long enough to take in the local culture? Snow sports? Mushing?"

"Wouldn't know where to start. Figured I'd begin with not freezing to death on the daily commute and take baby steps from there." Her quick grin caught him by surprise once again.

Recovering, he blurted, "Garage or block warmer?"

She peered at him and blinked. "Do what to the who now?" Her Southern accent flowed over him.

Unable to resist connecting with her, he rested his hand on her elbow for a split second. "Where did the hospital put you up?"

"Seems forward of you to ask."

"It's one of two rentals. The entire hospital staff, the town, and the surrounding villages all know where they are. It's not a secret." He ground his molars and extended his hands, palms up. "Reason I'm asking is that I want to get a sense of how much gear you need."

"Oh, okay. Sorry for getting defensive." Another flash of pain came and went, marring her attractive features.

He wanted to explore the story behind that expression.

She sighed. "I'm staying at the place on Second Avenue. No garage."

"Is there a white or black post about chest-high in front of the house?"

Her light brown brows drew together. "Yes."

"Engine block heater."

"Um."

He crossed his arms. "You don't know what that is, do you?" At her head shake, he said, "If you don't use the block heater, the cold weather is really hard on your vehicle. Engine might not start due to the oil becoming more viscous in the cold temps. Plug the vehicle in when you arrive in the evening and unplug when you leave in the morning."

"Where?"

"Oh boy." He pulled a picture of an engine block heater attachment on his phone. "The connection is usually on the front grille or a side recess on a sedan."

Her dark eyes went unfocused as she looked toward the ceiling. "Yes." She nodded. "I think I know where it is."

"Also, you'll need warmer outerwear. You will need to walk out to your car without freezing to death."

"Is that a literal risk or a figure of speech?"

"Both."

"Lordie." Her white teeth worried her lower lip, tempting Mav to taste.

Right there. He leaned an inch closer. She brushed her palms together, breaking his concentration.

Straightening her spine and patting her purse, she said, too brightly, "Okay, then. Let's get some better gear. Lead on."

He put a hand on her forearm, stilling her. "Why are you here, Lee?" He felt the tiny shudder even through her coat.

"I'm buying groceries and winter gear."

"No, here. In Yukon Valley."

A pause. "Filling gaps in critical access hospital coverage."

Shaking his head, he said, "You could do that anywhere." Another outsider on a temporary adventure assignment in Alaska.

Another pained expression creased her forehead for a second. "Seemed like a nice place to be."

"Bull. People come out here because they're drawn to the area and the self-sufficient lifestyle, they have a romantic notion of the Alaskan bush, or they're running from something."

Her mouth dropped open, then snapped shut in a determined line. Those brown eyes glimmered. "Is nosy psychoanalyst your side gig, for the times when you're not busy making assumptions about members of the healthcare team?" Sharp heat laced her words. Her neck and cheeks reddened.

Crap. "No, I mean, I'm sorry. I—"

She swallowed and said in a voice a few notes too high, "So. Any recommendations for snow pants and boots?"

Chapter Five

THE ONLY REASON Lee didn't have to deal with a call from Mom on Monday, her first night in Yukon Valley, after she'd gotten settled in the modest two-bedroom rental mostly had to do with the four-hour time difference between Georgia and here. Unfortunately, when Mom texted Lee Tuesday morning … *oof*, that loud *ding* hurt at five a.m. local time. At least she texted rather than called. Easier to deal with right now in the pitch-black chill of early morning.

When are you coming back home? Preston was asking about you. He's considering a run for city commissioner.

Lee pinched the bridge of her nose. No *how are you* or *did you arrive safely?*

Nope. In Mom's world, denial was indeed a river in Egypt. Ignore, avoid, distract—that was her go-to response when embarrassed. Mom had much more pressing items, like maintaining the family image. That meant wifey Lee needed to be seen supporting her ex.

Apparently, infidelity, sucking Lee's savings account dry, and a divorce didn't slow Preston Dupree down from brazenly climbing the local government career ladder like kudzu. He truly was a weed—nice-looking in season, useless, and relentless in its destruction of everything beneath it.

He sure enjoyed using her family's connections for a foothold. He'd also enjoyed the first several years of her attending physician salary. Holy heck, he had gone through those funds faster than a fresh ten blade on tensioned skin. In the divorce mediation, it was ironic how he insisted on sharing her money but not her medical school loan liabilities or the credit card debt. When faced with a future fifty-fifty split of her income *and* her debt, he'd agreed to call things square with what he'd already spent in lieu of her future earnings and walked away. She had her own income, own debt, and her very own rock-bottom credit rating. He had his Range Rover, a ski boat in its premium slip at exclusive Bald Ridge Marina on Lake Lanier, and their three-thousand-square-foot lake cottage on which they still owed a bushelful—all in his name now, including payments.

She typed back. *It's a three-month locums contract. And it's five in the morning.*

You never needed sleep. I'm up. It's nine in the morning here.

She sighed. Communication with Mom had little to do with Lee.

Another message. *Come back and help at the local practice in Alpharetta. See some patients a few days per week. You'll have time to join Beau Monde with all my friends.*

High on the list of things Lee didn't wish to do—enjoy monthly tea and tiny cakes during midmorning meetings of well-dressed ladies who voted on which charity their society dues should support, while planning the next fundraising cocktail party at the country club. Nothing wrong with Beau Monde, or any social philanthropy for that matter. But if Lee were back in Georgia, she'd feel more at home seeing patients, not brunching over small talk.

Didn't matter. Lee had no extra money for society dues or much else, thanks to Preston and his financial vacuum cleaner act. Which was unfortunate, given that she needed to get a few more work outfits and a new pair of shoes after ruining the ones she had worn in the snow yesterday. Wasn't like she could shop locally for clothes like that. In a few days, the Amazon Prime order would reach this rental house. Lee snuggled deeper into the blankets.

True, she could have fought Preston to get some of her money back, but those funds were long gone, spent on his toys and memberships. Also, Mom hadn't wanted their divorce to be public, so the less messy the resolution, the better. Mom constantly fretted about what this divorce meant for her affiliation with Beau Monde and for Dad's political image.

Lordie. What a situation. Which reminded her, by late next week she should get her first locums paycheck deposited in her bank account. Lee needed that small infusion of money flowing into a fresh new account Preston couldn't access to make a dent in her overdue credit card bill and stay on time with this month's student loan payment. Yay, only twenty-seven more years to go until her loan was paid off.

Her parents presented as wealthy, but Lee knew the truth. She'd gotten a merit scholarship for college and took out need-based loans to cover all of medical school. However, all their friends seemed to be under the impression that her parents had easily paid out of pocket for her education. Mom always said, "Successful people find a way to appear successful."

On the outside, the Tipton family sure did look the part.

Mom continued. *I can inquire with Dr. Lunsford. They'd hire you in a minute. No one needs to know about that little speed bump in your marriage. You could start fresh by helping Preston's campaign.*

Gritting her teeth, Lee pulled the blanket over her head, fighting to stay warm against the chill. Speed bump, her freezing butt.

Why would I want to go back to him? she replied. *He cheated and stole from me. He tried to get me fired on a made-up HIPAA violation. He's not a good person.*

Unlike a certain handsome and earnest EMT who, despite his gaffes, seemed like a genuinely kind guy whose main agenda appeared to involve helping others and making her heart rate speed up. Lee wouldn't mind spending some time with him in the back of his ambulance.

Sitting in the dark cocoon of blankets, she pictured his hands sweeping over her waist and back as her fingers traced the firm ridges of his chest and shoulders. His mouth would be warm as he nipped at her lips. Mmm. The shiver that skidded down her spine had nothing to do with the air temperature.

Nope. No rebounds. No do-overs. No saving face for her ex. No more trusting her ability to pick someone with honorable motives. Heck, she barely knew Maverick. He was a handsome guy who had been slightly kind to her. She shoved far out of her mind the image of his broad smile that reached to his bright blue eyes.

She reread her last text. Leave it to Lee's ingrained polite upbringing to describe that narcissistic, money-grabbing, philandering social climber of an ex-husband as *not a good person*. It was like saying traffic on I-75 through Atlanta was *a little busy*.

Everyone makes mistakes, Mom typed. *I'd rather keep your temporary separation private. Your father's reelection bid and Preston's career goals mean that we all need to do our part to help.*

Heaven forbid Lee tarnished her family's carefully cultivated image of wealth and success. That image was a façade, anyway. Her parents had inherited their home in Alpharetta from Grandpa Tipton, including all of the furnishings. They pooled the best fixtures in the most public spaces. Rooms with worn rugs or substandard furniture never hosted visitors. Simple as that.

Mom and Dad's mantra. If you refuse to see a problem, then the problem didn't exist.

Case in point. Lee's divorce.

No, the priority was Dad's aspirations, which meant achievement in local politics and projecting success in every aspect of his and his family's life. Mom's persona as a wealthy but charitable and supportive society wife needed to remain untarnished.

Lee sat up in bed. What part of *final divorce decree* did Mom not understand? The only reason last fall's dissolution of marriage paperwork had sailed through the court was her parents' connections with a judge who agreed to sign off— quietly—if Dad would consider the judge's sister's request for a business license to open a boutique in an area of

Alpharetta zoned residential. Lee wiped imaginary grease off her palms, thinking about yet another of Dad's back-door deals.

I have to go to work, she typed.

It's five in the morning. You don't have to leave for work. I haven't had my breakfast and newspaper yet.

Lee could imagine Mom in her flowy robe, sitting in the sunroom, sipping a fresh-squeezed orange juice, flipping through the lifestyle pages of the *Alpharetta-Roswell Herald*, and *tsking* about the goings-on of the area's upper crust.

Talk later. Lee would have thrown the cell phone if not for the fact that she was on call starting in three hours, which required a functioning means of communication. The pager was nice, but it helped to have a way to return the page to the hospital.

She flopped back and pretended that the modest but tastefully decorated rental house room was filled with warm filtered sunlight that dappled thick and shiny magnolia leaves. She imagined the pungent white blossoms moving in a warm breeze. If she screwed her eyes shut, she could envision bright red azalea bushes nearby.

Lee's nose was cold.

ON FRIDAY THAT week, Lee adjusted her green Max Mara blouse under her lab coat as she hurried from the inpatient area of the hospital to the clinic. Running late. Again. She waved at a smiling Deirdre Steen in passing and kept on speed-walking in her ruined leather shoes. The new ones she'd ordered had pushed her credit card balance to the limit, but with luck the shoes and a few other garments would be here soon. She smoothed a hand over her slacks and focused on her day's work.

Two new babies plus several adult patients with pneumonias, COPD flares, and one serious case of sepsis meant that today's rounds had started early and lasted until late morning.

Yukon Valley might be a small facility, but there was nothing small about the patient care here. She had worked in Dahlonega, Georgia, technically a rural facility, but her inpatient work there had been limited to laboring patients and newborns. A hospitalist team managed all of the inpatient cases, shipping out any severely ill patients. ER doctors treated ER patients. Outreach specialists visited frequently, making clinic and hospital consultations easier to access. Every doctor had a narrowly defined scope of practice.

Not so in Yukon Valley Hospital. Lee, the other two family doctors, and two physician assistants held the line here at the end of the world. They literally treated everyone and everything because there was no one else to care for the people living in this area. Not just the town but she'd been told the hospital also covered several Native tribes—no, she reminded herself, the tribes were called corporations here— within a sixty-mile radius.

Lee peered out the hospital's main entrance windows at the snow blowing sideways across the parking lot. On days like this, sending sick patients to Fairbanks or Anchorage wasn't an option.

She popped into the ER. No patients. No ambulances bringing patients in. No paramedics with broad shoulders and a broad smile.

Not that she was looking for anyone.

She headed to the opposite side of the facility, stepping through an unmarked door into the back entrance of the clinic. She slipped into the break room, nearly running over Dr. Kathy Moore, a rural physician who had thirty years of experience. Kathy yelped and curled her entire body around a steaming cup of coffee.

"Sorry!" Lee held her hands up.

"My precious." Kathy stroked the mug which read I HEART ATP on one side and had a picture of the Krebs cycle on the other. She straightened, took a sip, and sighed, the numerous lines on her face relaxing. "How's Ruth Sampson doing?"

Lee mentally reviewed the hospital census while eyeing the homemade treats on the table. Staff often brought in yummy snacks.

"Prednisone is helping the COPD exacerbation, but on the downside, blood sugars have become hard to control."

"Nothing a little sliding scale insulin won't fix," Kathy quipped.

"Ah, but then add in a smidge of likely sepsis on top of the COPD flare, because who wants something easy? Blood, sputum, and urine cultures are pending, so for now, I'm sprinkling her with IV pip-tazo and vancomycin until I can narrow the antibiotic coverage. Giving saline boluses to improve perfusion until, of course, she inevitably gets fluid overloaded—because that will be my luck." Lee paused as she poured herself a cup of coffee and added sugar. "Would you prefer to round on her this week? One of the nurses said she's kind of a VIP."

Each of the doctors took hospital call in blocks of up to a week at a time and part of that duty involved rounding on all of the hospitalized patients. Taking call in longer blocks provided continuity of care, which was better for patient safety and outcomes. But being on call for multiple days at a time? Not as restful for the doctors.

Kathy smiled and sipped her coffee. "Ruth is a local village elder who I have seen for many years." She leaned a hip against the break room table. "However, I'm enjoying the fact that right now my phone doesn't ring and my pager doesn't beep. It's been great having you here, picking up hospital rounds, taking weight off of our shoulders. Shay was relieved to know her maternity leave would be covered."

Lee smiled. She hadn't met Dr. Pitka yet, but all the staff seemed to adore her. "I'm sure she and her family are enjoying the time off."

"Hmm. Sure." Kathy seemed to slip around the comment. "Here's what I know is true: Getting up at three a.m. feels different at age thirty than it does at age fifty … something." She smoothed a tendril of slate-gray hair back behind an ear. "That's not to say Paul and I aren't available to help if you need us. Dial-A-Friend is an option at any time." Paul Burmeister was the other family physician here,

DR. ALASKA

younger than Kathy by ten or so years and married to a radiology tech who was from the area.

"Good to know." Lee picked a chocolate chunk cookie, bit into it, and hummed to herself as the rich semisweet chocolate melted on her tongue.

"If you ever want to stick around, we can always use excellent rural doctors. The more the merrier."

Lee chewed and swallowed. "That's nice of you to say."

After a moment, Kathy asked, "So. Any more EMS rescues on the side of the road lately?" She peeked at Lee over the rim of the mug. "With cute paramedics around?"

"Smooth, Kathy." Lee cursed how her cheeks warmed. "Don't you have clinic patients to see?"

"My 10:30 patient was Ruth." Kathy pointed at the clock on the wall. "She no-showed me because *someone* admitted her early this morning. I have nothing but time."

Great. "Has my start in Yukon Valley become local legend?"

"Oh yes. We love new people and funny stories!" Another sip. "Everyone's heard about your introduction to Yukon Valley and warm welcome from the EMS crew."

Lee's heart fluttered, like a young girl reacting to a crush. No. She would not let herself think about Maverick in any way aside from a professional one. She knew the value of learning from history. Lee had been fooled by a handsome face before. Besides, her work in Yukon Valley had an expiration date. "It's as if a person could run naked from one end of town to the other and back, and the rumor would still beat them to the starting point."

45

Kathy shoved up the sleeves of her thick sweater. "Well, the windchill out there *is* minus twenty, so I'd like a heads-up on the arrival of the naked person so we can properly treat their hypothermia and frostbite." She snagged a snickerdoodle from a plate and dunked it in the coffee before taking a bite. "Come on. Throw an old lady a bone. I don't get out much, so these sorts of happenings in town are always exciting. Besides, the guy who works at the deli—"

"Tuli?"

"Yes. He's Ruth Sampson's grandson, if you didn't know. If you've interacted with him or if someone mentioned you around him, then any rumors have already gone around town via his online posts. Twice. He's got more connections on social media than the national power grid has outlets." She whispered, "I heard that famous singer, Alissa, follows him and liked one of his The Real Alaska movies he posts on the Insta."

Lee snorted at Kathy's attempt to stay up-to-date on the social media jargon. "Great. New gal gets to be gossip fodder. The interior Alaska online communities hear all about it. Shenanigans go viral. I see how you all roll." Lee laughed as she walked with Kathy toward the clinic work area. "Sorry to disappoint, but there's not a lot of rumor meat on the bone here."

Chapter Six

MAV WIPED DOWN the EMS gurney and straps after delivering Bruce back to the emergency department late that Friday afternoon. Aggie had insisted that Bruce come back in after he suddenly became short of breath after shoveling snow. Initial telemetry and vital signs on the ambulance were normal. Better to be on the safe side and do further testing.

If Mav had thought Bruce hated going to the hospital earlier this week when he wrecked the truck, the older man really didn't appreciate his wife forcing him to get checked out today, as the constant lines of muttered curses attested.

At the end of the day, though, Bruce was more scared of Aggie than he was of the hospital.

Mav glanced up at the waiting room doors. Aggie should be here by now. He'd stop by and reassure her that Bruce was stable and being evaluated.

Louise had run over to the hospital cafeteria to visit with her best friend who worked in the food services department. Barring any emergency calls for the ambulance, Mav had time to kill.

He looked around the department but didn't see a flash of golden hair. Instead, he spied the health unit coordinator, or HUC, typing away with a bowed head, likely registering Bruce's admission. Two ED nurses on shift were busy getting updated vitals and performing their initial assessments.

Brown hair fluttered as his sister hurried toward him.

"Hi, Dee. How's it going?" he called.

"Good. It's been busy on med/surg. Phew. Helping to tuck in admits for the weekend. Quality improvement meetings. Typical Friday." She paused. "Are you ready for guests in a few weeks?"

The lodge they co-owned had been their parents' dream property for the past ten years. His parents had unknowingly bought it out from under another buyer, which had apparently created waves. Fair's fair—their bid was higher, and they were quicker to offer. They had happily picked up the property and enjoyed developing it, right up until they died in the bush plane crash several years ago.

Mav and Deirdre couldn't bear to let the property go, despite the mortgage. They'd even turned down increasingly insistent offers to purchase the lodge and acreage. Why here, in Yukon Valley? As long as Mav and Dee didn't default on the mortgage, the property and the business would stay in the family.

"I need to freshen up the cabin they'll use and fix a few loose boards on the steps to their front door. I'll prep extra lodge rooms in case there are more people in the party or they want additional space. Not like we're busy this time of year."

Truth. They were very much not-busy, and lack of business income led to lack of mortgage payments. It was a big problem he and his sister continued to grapple with.

She pressed her mouth into an unhappy line and avoided the obvious topic of lack of reservations. "The babies?"

His motley crew of retired sled dogs didn't know how to go for a leisurely walk without enthusiastically towing him through the woods. Although nowadays, some of the team preferred lounging by the fireplace.

"What about them?" He refastened the gurney straps so they wouldn't drag on the floor.

"They won't get in the way or bother the guests? We need happy customers." The corners of her mouth dipped. "We need repeat customers. Stat."

"The team is family. That's nonnegotiable. You're doing that micromanaging thing again, Dee."

"Some people don't like dogs."

His sister always had a vision of the property that landed closer to a Four Seasons than the humble but welcoming lodge home that included a wing of several modest guest rooms and collection of three cozy hewn-log cabins.

"People who don't like dogs are not the people I want in my life. Income or not, I'm not removing the dogs to suit our guests."

Those dogs had dragged his sorry butt through the Cold-foot 550 six years ago. When a blizzard hit, the team had saved his life, pulling hard despite the whiteout and somehow staying on the trail. The five dogs remaining from that team were family members, plain and simple. They deserved all the treats and belly rubs and as many naps in retirement that they wanted.

Deirdre raised her hands. "Suit yourself. But we're underwater. Occupancy was down during last fall's hunting season. Repairs are piling up and getting more expensive as time goes on. I don't want to do anything to dissuade repeat business or good reviews."

"You know my criteria. Must like dogs."

She sighed. "Is that for guests or for anyone in your life?"

"It's a general philosophy. I don't need anyone in my life."

"You sure about that, Mav?" Pinning him with a blue-eyed stare, she raised an eyebrow. "When are you going to start dating again? It's been more than two years since Skylar."

What a disaster. He had invested time and emotional energy, and for what? Hard lessons had been learned. He flicked his thumb along the edge of the gurney pad. "Dee, you seem busy at work. How do you have enough time to dissect my nonexistent love life? What about your relationship future?"

His sister crossed her arms and bristled. Uh-oh. Watching her wrath was like standing under a spring snow cornice. One good gust of wind to dislodge it, and he'd be pulverized and buried.

He started to sweat under the uniform layers, topped by the windproof EMS coat. His brother-in-law's death five years ago still stung. Dee had coped by throwing herself into her work. *Head down, keep busy*, as their parents often said.

Unbidden, an image of a certain person with sun-kissed cheeks and golden hair flashed in his mind's eye. Was he missing an opportunity by keeping his head down and staying busy?

Yet, he'd been burned more than once. This latest time with Skylar hurt. They had done the long-distance online dating thing. They got along. She was witty and nice. Adventurous. Outdoorsy. She thought she had wanted the Alaska experience with Mav and dove in feet-first.

The isolation and challenges that came with this stark landscape quickly drove a wedge of resentment between them. Mav had tried to provide her with as many amenities as he could afford, and some he couldn't afford. Still, he had done his best to make her comfortable. She didn't last more than a few months into winter before she fled back to Nevada. On her way out, she tore emotional strips out of him when she criticized the crappy location, the failing lodge business, Maverick's all-consuming EMT work that took him away from her side, and—worst of all—the smelly dogs.

"There's no one on the horizon, sis."

"You sure?"

He rubbed his chin as murmurs from the nurses and Bruce drifted back to him. He did not want to have this conversation. Not now and not here. He would bet twenty bucks that the middle-aged HUC's typing was completely random so she could eavesdrop on the conversation. "Why are you pushing?"

"It wouldn't be the worst thing for you to get out and see someone again. Be a normal human instead of burying yourself in EMS duties and running the lodge."

"That lodge isn't going to fail. I'll make sure of it."

"If you find the right partner."

"What?"

"Pick someone who brings something to the table, Mav. Who can help."

Was she suggesting being with someone because of money? No way. That was a cynical recommendation, even for Dee. "Come on. That's not how I roll."

"Two birds, one stone is all I'm saying."

"No way. Besides—" Before he could close his stupid mouth, he said, "Who do you suggest in this small town? There's not a lot of options, and certainly no one that can 'bring something to the table' in the way you're suggesting. Or should I try again with someone from the outside who can hack living out here?"

"I know exactly who I'd suggest. Might do you some good to get back in the game." She inhaled sharply. "Never m—"

"Sorry, but not going to happen. Not with *her*. Can you even imagine that delicate genius handling even a mild Alaska storm, much less being able to survive for any length of time out here? She'd probably break a nail deicing her car and then go running back to the lower forty-eight."

"Mav."

"That woman's idea of roughing it is setting the winter thermostat to sixty-four degrees. I know because I helped her shop for warm clothes, so she won't die out here."

"*Mav*," Deirdre hissed.

He shook his head. "Listen. Some people aren't cut out for this place or this kind of work. She'll be gone by mud season, if not sooner. If not, she's probably using the time to look for an Alaskan husband, like on the shows." That last bit came straight out of personal experience, damn it. He stopped talking.

Dee's eyes went round.

He froze.

Aw, hell no. Not again.

He turned around.

His gaze slammed into narrowed brown eyes that glittered. If Lee could shoot lasers by blinking, he'd be cut into a million pieces by now.

"I mean …" Glancing back at his ashen sister, he asked Deirdre, "Would it kill you to warn me that she's right there?"

Lee tapped the toe of her leather bootie on the floor and lifted her hands near her face. "*She* can hear you, and besides, you shouldn't be saying those things behind *her* back."

Mav opened his mouth, but no words came out.

The HUC watched with an avid expression, dropping all pretense of doing work. Mav had an audience. More grist for the rumor mill.

Deirdre moved into his direct line of sight. "Nice move there, bud." She smirked as she slinked away with a wave.

With a swallow, he turned to Lee. "I didn't mean what you think I—"

"You meant whatever you meant."

A pulse jumped in her neck, visible above the dark green shirt with a maroon stethoscope draped around the collar. For a split second, he wanted to rest his fingertips against the smooth skin visible above the subtle V-neck. What would her skin smell like, right there? Would it taste tart and sweet, like her scent?

Then she threw virtual ice water on him. "Your opinion of my staying power doesn't matter. For the record, you have no idea what I'm capable of surviving." She pointed, her finger trembling.

Damn. That statement, combined with a flash of pain in her eyes, made for an interesting tidbit he wanted to explore. If she ever spoke to him again.

He managed to unstick his tongue. "What are you doing here?"

She waved a hand in a one-hundred-eighty-degree arc with a dry laugh. "Literally, I work here. You brought in a patient. I'm on call for the ED. Here I am. In the ED. To do my job, which you can bet your booty is *not* to seek a husband." Her features twisted into another brief rictus of anger that knocked the air out of him for a second. She clenched and unclenched her hands, then stepped forward. "Now, if you don't mind, I'm going to do my job." Her nostrils flared as she glared up at him. "Which makes one of us. You'd best go do yours instead of jawing."

Oh crap.

The time had come to eat crow yet again. This apologizing had become a bad habit. "Dr. Tipton. Lee. Hey, I was … way out of line." Out of the corner of his eye, Mav spied the HUC tilting her head.

That lady watched them like a wolf tracking prey. This story was going to make the rounds before Mav returned the

EMS rig to the garage on the other side of the hospital parking lot.

"Out of line? You think?"

Geez. She didn't have to rub it in. Why did every interaction with this woman begin with him stepping in a pile of moose droppings and end by her chopping him down to size?

"My sister ribbed me, that's all. About me being a dumb bachelor and all."

"Didn't seem that you were the target of ribbing."

"That's not fair."

"That's what I heard."

He peeled off the beanie, ran a hand through sweat-dampened hair, paused, and crammed the beanie back on. "We've *really* gotten off on the wrong foot, Lee."

"Dr. Tipton."

He swore that the HUC gasped.

Hell. "Can I make it up to you? Take you out to dinner"—the next few words flew from his head and straight out of the hole in his face before he could stop himself—"since you don't know anyone here."

She took that moment to smile, turn, and greet by name the two ED nurses leaving Bruce's room and wave at the HUC. "You were saying?"

Shoving his hands into coat pockets, he heaved a big lungful of air. "I mean, it's neighborly of me to invite you for a meal."

A snort escaped her. "Now you're the Welcome Wagon?"

"Would it help me get out of this grave I dug myself?"

A faint smile curved her lips as she studied him. A blush climbed her neck and washed onto her cheeks. The world tilted, and he couldn't catch his balance. He stood up straighter and tried to appear unassumingly dashing or handsomely friendly, whatever that entailed. With Mav's luck, he'd appear constipated.

Lee blinked, breaking whatever spell she had on him. "Okay. I'm not doing this back-and-forth stupidity. I have a patient to see, and you surely have an ambulance to drive." She turned on her heel and clomped about ten feet before grabbing a dollop of antiseptic foam as she entered the trauma bay and greeted Bruce.

Mav shook his head. So, she hadn't said no to dinner. Right?

The HUC glanced up with a wink as she typed. Probably taking notes on Mav's inability to have a normal human conversation and documenting the smoking ashes of his pride.

Shift would be over soon. Mav couldn't wait to sit by the fire with his old sled dogs. At least *those* relationships were simple.

Chapter Seven

"CODE BLUE, ED room two," blared overhead on repeat as Lee speed-walked from the inpatient wing toward the ED, joining several staff heading in the same direction. What the heck? Bruce had been stable and getting ready to be admitted for observation at the upcoming seven p.m. shift change. His lab results were reassuring.

Maybe someone had hit the code button by mistake or accidentally pulled the alert cord in the ED restroom? Wouldn't be the first time that had happened.

Or had another patient recently arrived and coded? Could be. Lee hadn't looked at the census in the past fifteen minutes. If EMS was coming in hot or if it was a John Doe, the patient might not have been added to the patient list. She fingered her cell phone, ready to pull up the ACLS algorithm. In a critical situation, even the best-drilled protocols flew out the window. Good to have her peripheral brain backup.

She tallied her resources as she hurried down the hallway. Six forty p.m. on a Friday. Drs. Burmeister and Moore as well as one of the physician assistants were all off today. The remaining PA had finished up their clinic schedule a few hours ago. The nurse anesthetist or CRNA took hospital call from home. Lee peeked out of a window. Windblown snow swirled beneath parking lot lights. The CRNA wouldn't arrive quickly enough.

Swiping her badge to enter the ED, Lee paused. A radiology tech rumbled the portable x-ray machine to a stop outside of room two. In the hallway, a rolling phlebotomy cart with a lab tech standing ready next to it waited in the hallway. The ED HUC stood at the trauma bay door with a laptop computer on a stand, acting as scribe, and moved so Lee could enter the room.

Lee stumbled on her own footstep.

It was Bruce.

Lee pulled in a lungful of air. Time slowed down.

Monitors beeped all over the place, ringing out three quick high beeps and two lower, loud beeps, over and over. Insistent sounds of impending death. Not good. Tense, low voices filled the room.

ABC. Airway, breathing, circulation. She could do this. She could run this code.

One of the ED nurses, Clyde, did a limbo move to duck under oxygen tubing on the wall and step over cords to start bag-mask ventilation from the head of the bed. He pressed Bruce's jaw up against the mask to create a tight airway seal despite Bruce's beard hair. Bruce's chest rose with each squeeze of the green ambu bag.

An ED nurse, Amberlyn, stood on a footstool, performing CPR compressions. The day shift charge nurse for the inpatient unit ran in wearing the Lucas compression device backpack. She set it on the counter and began unpacking it.

Lee took another big breath and positioned herself at the foot of the bed, gripping the footboard for support. An attending physician would be helpful right about now. She quickly scanned the team around her. No luck. Not a cardiologist, ER doctor, or critical care specialist in sight, either. Damn it. She *was* the attending physician.

The sight of Bruce's pale face and lax body shot adrenaline through her, driving her to panic. Driving her to rush through the steps.

No. The words of Dr. Tyanna Ross, one of her OB fellowship attendings, floated up from several years ago when Lee was elbow-deep in emergency C-sections and high-risk deliveries. *Slow is steady. Steady is smooth. Smooth is fast.*

"Update." Lee projected her voice to stay calm but carry over the incessant and loud telemetry alarms.

Deirdre glanced up from where she knelt, placing a second IV line and drawing several tubes of blood. Keeping her eyes on her work, she said, "Chest pain started a few minutes ago along with increasing O2 requirement. Initial troponin level was normal. We were waiting on the four-hour repeat troponin before admitting him. Amberlyn"—she nodded toward the nurse doing vigorous compressions, her long, dark hair floating in front of her face—"was about to call you, but then Bruce said he felt 'something wrong in my chest.' He lost consciousness. Telemetry went from sinus to sinus tach, and about thirty seconds ago, it rolled straight over to V-fib." A quaver roughened her words.

She handed off the multiple vials to the lab tech, who hurried out of the room. Then she taped the IV in place with a deft flick of her wrist and stood.

Lee stared at the monitor that displayed small irregular waves. It beeped with alerts but emitted no sounds of regular heartbeats. Ventricular fibrillation—an unstable heart rhythm incompatible with survival. "Pulse?"

Clyde pressed on Bruce's neck. "Not palpable."

"Let's shock."

"Got it." Deirdre retrieved pads from the top drawer of the rolling CPR cart and slapped them on Bruce's hairy chest as Amberlyn restarted compressions.

"V-fib. Shockable rhythm," Lee confirmed once more, sweat prickling between her breasts. The likely cause of Bruce's collapse was cardiac, but she had to think through all reasons for the arrest. Pulmonary embolism, sepsis, cardiac tamponade, pneumothorax, electrolyte disturbances.

"Charge to one hundred twenty joules." Lee stepped away from the bed. "I'm clear." She scanned the room as Deirdre moved away from the metal railing.

Clyde lifted the ambu bag away from Bruce.

"You're clear." Lee checked once more as Amberlyn raised her hands and stepped back. "Everyone's clear. Shock."

Deirdre pushed the button, and Bruce's body jumped.

Lee studied the cardiac monitor pattern for ten seconds. "Still V-fib. Continue compressions and let's give one milligram of epi." Lee turned to the HUC. "Please tell me when it's been three minutes, and we will repeat the epi dose."

Deirdre grabbed the brown medication box from the

CPR cart, opened it, flicked the caps off the vial and syringe at the same time with both thumbs, shoved the vial into the syringe, then injected epi through the IV port.

Lee's response to stressful situations was objective and measured—going to pieces could wait for later. She pulled up the ACLS algorithm on her phone. "Continue compressions for two minutes." She confirmed that a bag of IV fluid ran at a wide-open rate. Unlikely to be volume depletion, but that was an easy diagnosis to treat, and the fluids might improve blood pressure.

Deirdre and another staff member slid a hard plastic piece under Bruce's back as Amberlyn continued her CPR efforts. In less than a minute, they had the Lucas automatic compression device set up and chunking out high quality, regular chest compressions. Panting, Amberlyn wiped sweat from her forehead, stepped away from the bed, and tucked the stepstool into the corner of the room.

Lee had less than two minutes to think during each CPR cycle. What came next? It had been several years since her training, and even then, the residents had in-house critical care, hospitalist, or emergency department docs to supervise codes. Lee had paid close attention and kept up her certifications, but Lordie, this situation stretched well beyond her comfort zone.

She squeezed her grip on the plastic footboard. "All right. Let's get an advanced airway. You up for it, Clyde?"

He eyeshot her a wide-eyed expression and gave a curt shake of his head. "Out of my scope of license. What about the CRNA?"

No one answered. Lee's palms got sweaty. The CRNA hadn't arrived yet. Criminelly. How long had it been since she had intubated an adult? Stiffening her spine, Lee covertly scrolled on her ACLS steps so she could select endotracheal tube and laryngoscope blade sizes without floundering.

She would have to do this herself. Okay, then.

"Anyone want some help?" a familiar low voice carried through the murmurs, telemetry beeps, and relentless grinding *chunks* of the pistoning Lucas device. Maverick filled the doorway, beanie and coat on, paramedic kit over his shoulder. Louise hovered next to him, dark brown eyebrows raised.

"Yes!" Lee and Deirdre said in unison. No idea how Maverick and Louise managed to be here, but in Lee's universe, the more qualified help she had, the better.

Maverick flashed a quick grin, looked down at Bruce, then shook his head. "For the record, he was fine when Louise and I dropped him off."

Deirdre glared daggers at her brother.

He raised his hands. "*Oof.* Tough crowd." He set the paramedic bag on the floor and opened it, shrugged out of his coat and hat, snapped on gloves, then unwrapped one end of the endotracheal tube sterile packaging and laid it next to Bruce's head on the bed. He pulled out a laryngoscope blade and snapped it open on the handle, making the blade's bright light shine. "Move that way for a second, Clyde."

"Two minutes," the HUC spoke up.

"Stop compressions," Lee said, studying the monitor for

a few seconds. "V-fib. Charge to one hundred fifty joules."

Deirdre pressed the button to charge the defibrillator, the high-pitched whine of the machine ratcheting up the stress level in the room.

"I'm clear. You're clear. Everyone's clear," Lee said. She double-checked that the metal laryngoscope Maverick held in his hand didn't touch the bed. "Shock."

Deirdre pressed the button, and Bruce's body jumped again.

After another few seconds, the monitors resumed the loud, wild alarms. "V-fib." Lee stared at the monitor. *Damn it.* "Pulse?"

Clyde checked. "Not palpable." He continued bag-mask ventilation.

Her mind spun. *Focus on the ACLS steps.* "Resume compressions."

Amberlyn restarted the Lucas, and the device's thick *chunking* provided strange percussion to the high-pitched beeps from the telemetry machine.

"You good to intubate, Maverick?"

"Almost, Doc." He crouched, then picked up the laryngoscope.

"Three minutes, doctor," the HUC called out.

"Push another milligram of epi." Lee glanced at her phone. "Also, mark it so I remember to give three hundred milligrams of amiodarone IV in two minutes."

"Epi is in," Deirdre announced. "Pulling up three hundred milligrams of amiodarone to have ready."

The Lucas machine continued chugging away. Lee's

clenched jaw ached as she scooted around the bed, standing near Bruce's chest and ready to take additional action if needed.

Maverick's broad shoulders rose and fell once, twice. Then he braced his legs wide, bent down, and slid in the laryngoscope blade to move Bruce's tongue out of the way and lift the jaw. The only sound in the room was erratic, blaring alarms and the *chunk-chunk* beat.

Without taking his eyes off the blade, he said, "Louise, cric pressure."

Louise pressed her gloved thumb and index finger down on Bruce's cricoid cartilage, making the larynx structures easier to see and access during intubation. With her other hand, Louise held the sterile packaging as Maverick grasped the endotracheal tube. Once the tube was inserted, Louise removed the metal stylus inside the ET, or endotracheal, tube while Maverick held the ET tube in place. They performed the procedure without saying a word. Perfect teamwork.

With the ambu bag attached and Mav providing ventilation, Lee listened with her stethoscope over Bruce's chest. Bilateral breath sounds, equal chest rise visible. "ET tube placement looks good." She exhaled along with several other staff members in the room.

"It's been two minutes, Doc," the HUC said.

"Give amiodarone three hundred milligrams." She paused as Deirdre gave the medication. "Any test results yet?"

The HUC punched an extension into the portable

phone, mumbled, then shook her head. "Labs are still in process."

CPR continued. Maverick gave Lee a tight smile as he inserted the CO_2 detector for a few breaths, nodded, removed it, then reconnected the ET tube to the ambu bag that Clyde squeezed. Then he secured the endotracheal tube in place with tape.

Lee checked the monitor for the hundredth time. *Damn, damn, damn.* Time slowed. Her focus sharpened as she processed every detail around her. As Lee fought to stay calm, her words became slower and more deliberate, syllables drawn out. Those extra milliseconds gave her space to think.

To plan a few steps ahead. "Hold compressions." She peered at the monitor. Still in V-fib. "Let's go ahead and shock at two hundred joules, please." Lee crossed her fingers and tossed up a silent prayer.

She was running out of options to save Bruce's life. The longer he had CPR without return of spontaneous circulation, the less likely he was to survive.

Lee's mind raced. Her stomach tensed.

Deirdre charged the unit. "Come on, Bruce," she murmured, a shimmer in her eyes.

Maverick peered at his sister, one brow raised.

Everyone got clear on Lee's command.

Please work. A bead of sweat rolled down Lee's temple. Her dry mouth formed the word.

"Shock."

Deirdre hit the button. Bruce's body jumped.

One second.

Two.

Three.

Lee's gaze landed on the suddenly silent telemetry monitor, back to Bruce with the ET tube and IV lines, and then to Maverick. He gave her a reassuring nod, then resumed ventilating with the ambu bag. Amberlyn's finger hovered over the switch to restart compressions.

Then, regular beeps filled the room. Lee blinked. What? She pressed the back of her forearm to her damp brow and squinted.

Someone in the room muttered, "Whoa."

Telemetry read—oxygen saturation 95 percent, pulse sinus rhythm at ninety beats per minute.

"Oh my gosh," Lee said, her ears ringing. "Check for a pulse."

Clyde pressed his fingers against Bruce's neck. "Palpable and steady."

"Wahoo!" Amberlyn gave a gentle whoop.

Happy murmurs added to hers in the strangely quiet room. Only the regular, softer beeps of the monitor and the soft *whoosh* of the ambu bag filled the space now.

"Everyone agree?" Lee gripped the railing of the bed and leaned forward, scared to take her eyes off the monitor.

She doubted herself for a split second. Then she glanced over at Maverick.

He gave her a sheepish grin. "Hey, I'm just a paramedic, not a fancy doctor, but it looks like normal sinus rhythm to me. Ow." Maverick winced as Deirdre—carefully, since he was still providing ventilation—punched him in the arm.

"What?"

Lee palpated Bruce's carotid and felt the regular pulse. His chest rose and fell.

Her body felt boneless, and she exhaled. "Wow. Good job, everyone. Let's run a post-arrest epinephrine drip at"— she sized him up and did a quick math calculation— "twenty-five micrograms per minute."

Maverick's sky-blue gaze at the head of the bed locked on to Lee. Her face tingled. Probably residual reaction due to stark fear for Bruce's life. For what felt like way too long, she held still and studied Bruce.

Deirdre said, "Okay for me to remove the Lucas?"

"Yes, but ... send it with transport?" Lee's brain whirled while they took away the equipment and reattached EKG leads.

"No need. We have one on the bus." Maverick cleared his throat. "So ..." He drew out the word. "Next steps. We're thinking transport?" He wasn't ordering or directing. He worked as a team member, nudging her toward the correct answer.

Heck, yes. Bruce needed to be out of her ED, stat.

Her head bobbed. "He can't stay in this facility. We don't have an ICU or ventilator here." She thought through the unfamiliar resources out loud. "He needs to be in Fairbanks for critical care and cardiology management."

"Louise, could you call the evening shift EMS crew?" Maverick asked. "We have a transport vent on our rig." He paused. "Um, did you want a chest x-ray? Sedation during transport?" Throughout his questions, he kept squeezing the green ambu bag, creating steady, even breaths for Bruce.

Damn it. Her knees shook. She needed to focus on post-resuscitation stabilization.

Her thought processes took a while to catch up. "Yes. Absolutely. Portable chest, please." The radiology tech outside the room acknowledged the request and set up the machine. Lee then turned to Deirdre, who was holding open doors for the tech's machine. "Do you have Precedex in-house?"

She closed one eye and looked up at the ceiling. "Nope. Go fish. Got a second-choice sedating med?"

Lee's heart pounded. She checked the ACLS app on her phone. It didn't hold this answer.

She racked her brain, aware of seconds ticking along with the regular telemetry beeps. "Propofol?" Anything to provide sedation while he was intubated. Once he was evaluated further in Fairbanks, he could then be extubated in a safer setting.

"Bingo!" Deirdre quipped. "Back in a sec." She hurried to the ED's Pyxis medication dispenser in the center of the ED.

The radiology tech and Amberlyn slid the film cassette under Bruce's upper back, with Maverick maintaining the ET tube and airway. The tech squinted at Maverick and the ambu bag, then draped a protective lead apron over his neck and shoulders, covering him to his upper thighs. The whole time, Maverick continued to ventilate Bruce.

Lee and everyone else but the lead-aproned tech and Mav stepped out to avoid radiation exposure while the machine whirred and beeped.

Reentering the room, Lee pulled up the digital image on the portable x-ray machine's screen. ET tube in proper position. No pneumothorax. Cardiac silhouette was normal. No significant infiltrates in the lungs.

After the portable x-ray machine was trundled away, Deirdre hung the Propofol drip. Sedation was on board.

Lee shifted from foot to foot, every cell in her body wanting Bruce out of this hospital and at the larger Fairbanks facility. Now.

Maverick lifted his chin toward the trauma bay door. "Any day now with that transport vent, Louise. I'm getting carpal tunnel here."

His partner rolled her eyes and indicated for everyone to move so she could set up the equipment.

Lee gripped the bed railing. Next steps. *Think.* The on-call CRNA, Thomas, arrived, a perplexed expression crossing his face when he spotted Maverick and Louise and their equipment.

"I missed the party." He pulled a fur-lined hat with ear flaps off, revealing his close-cropped hair.

"Tom, could you scroll through the telemetry leads for me?" Lee asked.

Because if she knew one truth of medicine, it was that the doctors should never touch the monitors, vent settings, or the IV pumps, else they risked dirty looks or dismemberment by the rest of the healthcare team. Tom turned the dials, cycling through to show the readouts from available leads. It was like reading the EKG without needing to run a formal EKG. A quick way to get big-picture information.

"There." She pointed. "Tombstone." Lee used the expression to describe the characteristic EKG appearance in the early phase of an acute heart attack.

Maverick whistled low.

Deirdre winced and patted Bruce's arm. "Oh, Bruce." She quietly sniffled and met Maverick's eyes for a split second.

Lee ran through her cardiac anatomy. There was likely an occlusion somewhere along the watershed of the left coronary artery. Hopefully, Bruce would remain stable until he reached Fairbanks where the cardiac cath lab could open the blockage. Unfortunately, her patient needed the cath lab now. LifeMed helicopter or fixed-wing couldn't fly in this weather. Even if the ambulance could safely speed, he wouldn't receive intervention for at least three hours. Time was heart muscle, as they said.

The HUC's portable phone rang. After a moment, she turned to Lee. "Lab's calling with a critical result. Troponin is now elevated at 0.15."

Troponin. A marker of heart damage. The levels rose as more heart tissue was starved of oxygen.

No surprise. "Got that number for Fairbanks?" she asked the HUC.

Lee grabbed a seat in the central work area of the ED to call. Ten minutes of discussion included tips by a helpful critical care doc along with the on-call cardiologist in a three-way conversation. They walked through the plan for Lee to administer the clot-busting medication TPA. It would be the first time she'd done that by herself.

Here she was, truly practicing full-scope rural medicine at the end of the world. Completely on her own.

Only, she wasn't alone. Nurses and techs had come running to help with the code. The whole team made this work.

Lee waved Deirdre and Amberlyn over. "We need to give TPA and then send him on to Fairbanks."

Deirdre tapped her lip as the three of them walked back into the trauma bay together. "Amberlyn, if you can get the protocol checklist, I'll pull the TPA."

The way Deirdre remained calm was impressive. Lee quivered inside like a southern rattlebox seed pod in the fall.

"I'm assuming they want us to drip and ship?" Deirdre was saying.

Aka administering the dose while Bruce was en route to the heart center.

"Yes," Lee said.

"Not a problem, Dee," Maverick said, securing the transport vent tubing. "The dream team of Hilda and Moose know what to do." He lifted his chin at the two new medics who arrived.

Louise and Maverick huddled with their colleagues to give a report, their voices murmuring medical shorthand that Lee only half heard.

Lee stared at Bruce, now connected to the transport ventilator Tom was monitoring, the hisses and whooshes syncopating various beeps. Gently patting Bruce's sheet-covered leg, she sighed. She had to talk with his wife. Aggie was waiting in the family room outside the ED. One of the environmental services staff who was a friend of Aggie's had apparently dropped what they were doing to keep her company.

Another huge sigh escaped Lee as she smiled at the team around her. "Whew. Anyone else want to pass out, or is that just me?"

Everyone raised their hand, and she got a few grim laughs. Someone suggested going for drinks.

If only. Lee's call continued until Monday morning.

"Okay," she said to the team members still present. "Last time I'll ask. Anything else that we've missed? Anything else we need to do before transport? TPA's started along with the other drips, and he's tolerating them well. Weather issues?" she asked Maverick and Louise, who stepped back as the newly arrived medics prepped their equipment.

The new medic, presumably Hilda, shook her head. A beanie covered her hair, but some red strands escaped at the nape. "Every day is an iffy weather day in Yukon Valley. Don't worry. Moose here will get us to Fairbanks."

If the petite paramedic didn't look like anything like a Hilda, her tall, thin partner who Lee judged to be around fifty didn't look like a typical Moose.

Hilda continued, "I have zero desire to deal with another cardiac arrest on the bus ride." She and Moose worked with the rest of the team to move Bruce to the EMS gurney. They quickly secured him, and Hilda tapped the TPA IV bag and crossed herself before patting the gurney handles. "Let's boogie, Moosey."

Her partner shook his head as they exited. Louise followed behind them with a backward glance at Maverick.

Lee spun in a slow circle in the silent and still trauma bay, her ears ringing. Wads of packaging, plastic needle caps, IV luer lock caps and stopcocks, and a small puddle of saline fluid littered the floor.

A full-body shudder ran through her. She'd taken care of what needed to be done. Barely.

The team had performed amazingly well, despite not having any specialized staff available. Wow.

Training was one thing. Real world practice without any safety net was something else entirely. Lee had never truly experienced something like this situation before. Never known the terror of being the very last line of defense between life and death. In every way, this situation was as different from her practice in Georgia as it could be. Foreign. Cold. Uncomfortable, like leaning backward over a cliff while trusting a safety rope to hold. She swallowed against a hard lump in her throat.

No time to process. Lee needed to talk with Aggie.

Maverick stepped in the room, zipped his medic bag, and stood, hefting the bag over a shoulder.

"Hey." His low voice warmed her as he squeezed her upper arm. "You did good today, Doc."

Chapter Eight

MAV SENT LOUISE home, as their shift had ended. He had paperwork to complete, so he remained in the ED and finished his notes then went to restock their kit.

For some reason, Maverick didn't want to leave the ED. Not yet.

Because of paperwork.

He lifted his head as the ED doors swung open. It was just Clyde heading back in to grab his winter gloves he'd forgotten.

Huh. Mav wondered how Lee liked her new glove liners and mittens he'd picked out for her earlier this week. The only reason that thought came to mind was because he was a nice guy welcoming the new doctor to town. Being welcoming. And nice. That was all.

He clicked through the fields on the EMS form and rubbed his chin. He glanced at Dee, who sat across from him at the desk, typing away on her desktop, her usual efficient self. Taking another peek at the closed ED doors, he shifted in his seat. Dee paused, leaned around her monitor, and stared at him with a bland expression. Then she made a *mmm-hmm* sound and sat back, continuing to type.

Mav worked very hard to ignore his sister. Instead, he

listened to the light sounds of the empty ED. An environmental services employee cleaned the floors. The night shift nurses chatted as they restocked the trauma bay supplies.

Man, he hoped Bruce would be okay. Lee had done a great job directing the team. Mav knew that wide-eyed expression—she had wanted nothing to do with that code. He'd seen that expression before in EMS trainees. He'd seen it in nurses and docs who sometimes floated through town to cover for a month at a time, then fled after they realized the seat-of-the-pants situation out here. As Mav's ex had said, *not as advertised in the glossy brochure.* Hey, he'd done remote EMS runs where he had ended up over his head in a critical situation. He knew what fear felt like when it came to a dying patient.

How Lee was holding up? Despite her discomfort, she had remained calm during the crisis and took everything in stride, unlike some healthcare providers who got flustered and missed key steps.

Maybe she still wanted to grab that dinner he'd offered. She hadn't outright rejected him. Was that disaster of a conversation only a few hours ago? He ran his hand through his unruly hair, then tried to pat it into order.

How was he thinking about a date now? After finishing up a code where someone almost died?

Because Mav worked in healthcare. Compartmentalization was a job requirement.

He looked around the ED once more.

He drummed his fingers, typed, then deleted. Wrong box filled out. He rubbed his eyes and thought through everything he had to do this weekend.

Man, he had to get home and feed the babies. Also needed to ensure the lodge rooms and guest cabin were prepped for the snowmachiners. Take care of a few repairs. That meant digging out various paths to and from buildings, thanks to the ongoing, recent snowfall. Too much to do and no time for any of it.

Except for a little time to have dinner with …

Rubbing his neck, he rolled his head back and forth.

Dee peeked over again and sucked a tooth.

"What?" he shouted.

"Touchy much?" She batted her eyes at him.

Dee might have been thirty-six to his thirty-four, and they were both adults, but she still got way too much pleasure out of pushing his buttons.

"Fine," he grumbled, trying again—and failing—to concentrate on the EMS form.

"That's not an answer to my question."

"Why are you still here, Dee? You're, like, the boss. It's Friday. Your work is done. Go home."

She rolled her eyes. "Mav, I don't leave here. When there are holes in staffing or the need for an extra set of hands, it's my job to help out."

"But it's not your job, really." He might poke at his sister, but in truth he worried about how much she worked.

"It is out here."

"You're not using it as an excuse to avoid other things?"

After a pause, she scowled. "Are we playing this game? Do you want me to psychoanalyze you right here, right now?

Because I will do it."

"Hell no." He conceded the win to his sister and pushed back from the desk. "Back in a bit, then I'm heading out."

"Where are you going?"

Big sisters.

He rolled his eyes. "Restroom. Do I have your permission?"

"*Hmmph*," she said. "You should go to the doctors' lounge and use that one."

"Why?"

Her broad smile made him want to pop her in the arm. "For good reason."

"Quit matchmaking, Dee!" he bit out.

But sure, the lounge would be a good place to find … a restroom.

"Not matchmaking, Mav." He didn't buy the innocent expression. "Johan had mentioned that the main restroom is out of order for a bit."

"Oh. Then I'll use the ED ones."

Thumbing behind her, she said, "And Johan started cleaning them a minute ago." She waggled her fingers, irritating him, like when they were in elementary school.

Over the years, Dee had honed her skills for poking until Mav would lose his cool. Felt like manipulation. After a long day at the end of a long week, he was too tired to argue.

He tipped an imaginary hat at Dee as he strolled through the ED doors and hung a left toward the inpatient wing.

The hospital at nine p.m. on a Friday was nearly empty. Night shift nurses were busy doing rounds on their patients.

Visitors had left.

He badged into the door next to the DOCTORS' WORK ROOM sign.

The space held a small couch, recliner, coffee table, computer desk, fridge, and kitchen table with a few mismatched chairs.

It also held an unhappy doctor, judging by the slump of her shoulders and the frown.

"Knock, knock," he said out loud.

"Oh." Lee turned her head and rubbed her hands over her face, but not before Mav spied a glimmer in her light brown gaze.

In the space of a breath, he switched gears from work to ... something else. His arms itched to wrap around her. Provide comfort. Support.

What about more?

He would not answer dumb hypothetical questions.

She sat up straighter, shoving her long hair away from her face as she reached for her lab coat on the arm of the couch. "Does someone need me in the ER?" she said, pulling professionalism around her like armor, her jaw stiff.

"No. You're good." He hovered a few feet inside the room. At the end of the day, she looked like she could use a friend. "Ah, mind if I take a break with you?"

Lee's shoulders rose and fell as she scooted over. The vee of the shamrock-green shirt emphasized the smooth line of her neck.

He swallowed. "Is this an exclusive restaurant or can anyone dine here?" He pointed at her makeshift meal.

Lee blinked, then waved a hand at the paper napkin with a half-eaten snack and an apple juice cup on the coffee table in front of her. "May I interest you in the chef's special? All-natural artisan flatbread with a peanut reduction garnish paired with a late-harvest fruit cocktail?"

"A peanut butter packet and stale crackers?" He grinned, then wandered over to the counter with a basket full of packaged cookies, chips, and crackers that the dietary services staff stocked. He held up two packets of fig bars with a flourish. "I believe I'll try the free-trade fruit compote wrapped in organic pastry dough. Let me get one for you as well."

Her posture relaxed on a light snicker that made his heart thump. "Perhaps you would like to hear the beverage specials?"

Mav dropped onto the couch next to her, handing her one fig package and leaning forward to plate his bar on a folded napkin set at perfect right angles. "What do you recommend, garçon?"

Pursing her lips, she held an arm up as if a make-believe napkin were draped over it. "For you, sir," she intoned, raising her light brown eyebrows, "I recommend the vintage Shasta lemon-lime cola. It's like drinking a tropical sunrise with delicate undertones of ultrasound gel and chemical disinfectant."

"Tempting. Do you have something that will pair with my heartier dessert?"

"Ah, sir, I can tell you have a discerning palate." Her fingertips grazed his forearm as her eyes sparkled.

Mav's stomach took a nosedive. A basic instinct drove him to make her smile and touch him again.

She continued, "In that case, may I suggest the house reserve Shasta root beer. It tastes exactly like filling out paperwork feels like. Emptiness with a numb aftertaste of despair that lingers without satisfying." Lee kissed her fingers. "Magnifique."

"Shastalicious." Mav crossed the room to open the refrigerator, pulled out a plain Shasta cola, and returned to the couch. "I prefer a beverage that embodies professional suffering that is raw and underpaid, without any hope whatsoever of the sweet, sweet release of retirement."

She choked back a laugh, then eyed his drink choice with brow-raised disdain. "Shasta cola. So plebian." A sniff. "I suppose I'll allow you to dine with me."

A laugh came up from his gut. "Good to know you'll lower your standards."

Her smile froze, then dropped.

Mav's neck muscles tensed. Somehow he'd hit a nerve. He wanted to find out what caused that pain, but this wasn't the appropriate time or place.

"Cheers." He lifted the small can of soda and thumped it against her flimsy apple juice cup.

They ate in thoughtful silence for a few minutes until the space between them changed from companionable to awkward.

When he finished his snack and wiped his mouth, he leaned back against the couch cushion and halfway faced her. "How'd Aggie take the news?"

Lee propped her elbows on her knees, folded her hands in front of her, and rested her chin on the fingertips. "Those are difficult conversations, and they take a lot out of me. They're hard for the family, of course. As I'm explaining the situation, I always think about what else I could have done better with the situation." With a sigh, she sat back, lacing her fingers together on her lap and turned toward him. "She's a tough lady. Aggie was half worried and half mad, because—and I quote—'If I'm the only one who cares about that big galloop's health, then someone's spending too much time and energy.' I mean, she's got a good point."

"Bruce is a known mess, but he's *our* mess. We'll keep him duct-taped together."

"Fair. Aggie was also worried about traveling to Fairbanks. She's got her own health issues, and it's hard for her to get out in the cold weather to drive. I told her that the doctors and nurses there would keep her updated, and she could go tomorrow when roads are better and she's more rested. She was going to contact her son and let him know what was happening. He'll try to catch a flight to Fairbanks if the weather lets him. Apparently, he's an ER doc in Seattle, so it'll be good for Bruce to have a family member who understands the situation and what Bruce needs to do to recover."

"That's Calvin. He grew up here. Bruce isn't going to appreciate the medical expertise. He's likely to give Cal an earful." It had been years since Cal had been back. The guy might get an earful from some other folks in town, as well. "God willing, Bruce survives to complain another day." The silence in the room spread out like a warm blanket. "Hey, did you have time for a debrief?"

"With the team after the code? Informally. Why?" She made to get up, and he gently squeezed her forearm to still her. "Do you want to provide feedback?" she said as the corners of her mouth dropped again.

She eased back onto the couch. The way she said the last word indicated that *feedback* meant *criticism*.

"Hey. My only comment is that you did a great job tonight." He turned, moving his arm to drape over the couch cushions, wanting to be close but not crowd her. "That situation was not a guaranteed win."

A flicker of doubt furrowed her forehead, and she finally answered. "Felt like a fish out of water."

"You're a doctor no matter where you practice. You have the training, and when it came time, you knew what to do."

"With help."

"No one does this work on their own, Doc. Not even a cocky paramedic who thinks he knows it all."

She paused. "Lee."

Mav held her gaze. "Do I have first-name permission now?"

Her gaze softened. "As you said, we got off on the wrong foot. I got defensive and leaned on rank."

"I was out of line with my big mouth. Besides, it's your rank to throw around."

She rubbed her eyes. "That's not true. You're right in saying that everyone has a job to do here. And every job is critical. Obviously. Patients do well when everyone works together."

With a flash of need, Mav wanted to be the one smoothing those tired furrows between her brows. To what end? Her job here was temporary. Mav didn't do temporary. He didn't do fish out of water, as she put it. He'd learned that lesson and then some.

He *did* do healthcare colleague support. "Some roles have higher levels of responsibility. We might be a team, but you're the quarterback."

"Hmm. Does that make you the running back?"

He pretend-flexed an arm and swaggered while sitting. "Tight end, probably."

A bright sunshine laugh burst out of her. "You're not wrong." Then a red blush crept up her neck and cheeks as she glanced down then up. "Oh my. Welp." The laughter faded.

Huh. His chest warmed and he drank in view of her pink cheeks and sparkling eyes. "You seemed very composed in that trauma bay."

"Like a duck swimming, calm on the surface and paddling frantically underneath the water."

"If you had nerves, you hid it well. Although—"

Sucking in a breath, she pulled back. "What?"

"Couldn't help but notice that your words got longer and longer the further into the code we went. That accent became more pronounced."

Scowling, she said, "That's my tell. The worse the situation gets, the slower I talk. One-syllable words become three-syllable words."

"Even bad words?"

"Especially those!" They chuckled together, and she rested her head against the couch cushion.

His fingers brushed her golden hair. Just a small touch.

One corner of her mouth rose. "The drawl didn't stick out as much when I was in Georgia."

"So that's where you're from? I guessed Alabama."

She made a smelled-something-bad face that drew another chuckle from deep in his gut. It had been way too long since Mav had relaxed and laughed.

A few seconds later, her sigh washed over him like a warm breeze as she murmured, "Guess I'd best write up my notes from Bruce's code. Check on my other patients before leaving for the night." The professional armor fell back into place.

"Lee."

Her head whipped up.

He breathed in the light floral and berry scent that was uniquely hers. "Everyone has to take time to crack a little bit. Let out the pressure."

"But I'm supposed to be an example. Strong. Steady."

"Doesn't matter who you are on the team. It's important. No one is an island, as the saying goes."

"Are you saying that you also ... crack?"

His days of trying to act tough were long past him. Mav had years of experience in the field. He'd seen his fair share of disasters and miracles, including the heartache that came with some cases. Part of the issue with being the EMS director was similar to what Lee was going through. He had to remain strong for the team, but Mav had learned that his job also included good mental health habits. "Everyone has a breaking point. The trick is letting the stress out as things happen, bit by bit, and not stuffing it away to explode later."

"I'm not a ticking time bomb."

"I'm no munitions expert. But I do know when someone might need a friend. Or an ear." He met her gaze. "Or a hug."

Lee froze.

Chapter Nine

LEE'S HEART SCAMPERED while her brain reminded her to breathe. When was the last time someone had cared about her well-being? Hugged her? Touched her in a way that made her feel safe and supported? Oh sure, her mom and dad gave her hugs at the airport when she left for this assignment, but truth be told their arms were full of disappointment.

Mav pulling her into an embrace? Ever since she'd met him at the highway crash, a part of her wanted to know what it would feel like to press against that broad chest. Did his arms feel as strong as they appeared?

It's too soon, a little voice in her head piped up.

Unprofessional, another internal voice said.

You misjudged a man before, she reminded herself.

One hug won't hurt, she argued, craving the human touch and release of stress along with the man.

What did she know about him? Mav seemed like a normal guy who worked hard and wanted to help others. Nothing he'd done suggested he would play games or use her for some ulterior motive. Did he feel sorry for her, like, *hey, here's the new doctor all shaky after a sketchy clinical situation?* Maybe he simply wanted to prop her up so she survived this locums assignment—in the interest of patient care.

She studied his earnest sky-blue gaze and didn't read pity there. The firm press of his mouth into a determined line tempted her to ease forward, make a connection, allow herself to lean on someone for a moment.

That act took trust—not in Maverick but in herself.

"Apologies." He grimaced. "Just letting you know I'm here, Lee. Nothing more than that." Out of the corner of her vision, his hand on the couch opened as he stretched fingers toward her. Then he rolled the hand into a fist and dropped it on his thigh. "Sorry if my saying so wasn't appropriate." Disappointment dropped the tone of his voice, and he pushed to his feet with a creak of pleather and a stiff *shush* of his uniform fabric.

"No, I'm ..." What was she? Lee was a Southern woman desperate to feel warmth in the Arctic. The chilliness had nothing to do with geography and everything to do with her past and her present colliding in front of her. "Yes. Sure."

"Yes, what?"

She swallowed a hard lump. "I'd appreciate that hug. Professionally speaking."

He held his arms a few inches away from his body, hands open. Other than that, he didn't move.

Lee stood. Her line of sight fell right at the vee of his navy EMS button-down shirt. The muscles of his neck tensed and relaxed. He remained still.

She had to take the first step. Ask for what she needed. Take the support offered.

Trust that he wouldn't hurt her.

Trust herself.

Lee stepped up, her feet fitting between his shoulder-width spaced ones.

Heat poured off of him. She inhaled his scent of cold, fresh air and a hint of spruce trees.

Mav didn't move. One of his hands shook.

"It's okay?" she breathed, not able to meet his gaze.

His chest rose and fell in front of her. "Very okay."

Sliding her arms around his waist, she rested her cheek against his upper chest. With a deep hum, Mav closed a circle behind her, lightly pressing his palms against her stiff spine. The rapid thud of his heart under her ear rivaled her own heart rate.

After a full minute—or was it an hour?—the joints in her body loosened and she relaxed into him, breathing in his warm scent. Under her fingers, his hard back muscles bunched up tight—strength held in check, like an engine revved but remaining in neutral.

It had been far too long since she'd leaned on someone. Too long since she enjoyed simple human connection. Tears prickled her eyes, and she suppressed a sniffle.

"Lee." His low voice transmitted from his sternum into her cheekbone.

Solid. Warm. His broad chest felt like a safe shelter in a blizzard. His arms telegraphed support. His lips …

His lips?

Another shift of his embrace and a dip of his head preceded a whispery brush of his mouth against her hairline. He did it again. Wonderful sparks of pleasure followed the path of his lips down to her temple.

She pulled back to look up at his sky-blue eyes that had darkened. Pupillary dilation. Signaled interest.

She licked her lips.

How dark had her eyes become?

Lee raised her head, so his lips fell on her cheek in front of her ear. A frisson of excitement zipped down through her chest and settled low in her pelvis.

Maverick used his chin to ease her head farther to the side and then gave her earlobe a gentle lick. The sensation and his breath feathering her skin triggered delicious warmth that radiated out from deep inside of her.

"Oh." She exhaled, curling fingers into fists on his back.

He slid one hand up to bury his fingers in her hair and cup the back of her head. Then he tugged, and an answering pull pulsed between her legs. Was this truly happening? Lee was waking up, like she'd hibernated in a numb state for months and months and finally rejoined the world. *Is this okay?* she checked in with her innermost self.

Not only okay but welcome. She wanted more of whatever *this* was.

No. It wasn't the actions she craved but the person.

Maverick swallowed, his Adam's apple bobbing. Muscles of his arms and chest bunched and shifted around her. "Um, not to be too—" The cords of his neck shifted again, as if forming words took effort. He stared at her lips. Licked his own. "But I'd like to—"

"Me, too." Lee rose on her toes to close the space between them, a hot, sparking connection.

His firm lips were velvet, and he moved over hers, constantly changing angles and pressure. He licked and nipped at the corners of her mouth and the bow of her upper lip until she gasped. Had she actually made that sound?

His hand on the back of her head tightened, holding her in his blissful grasp, his other arm locked around her waist. The temperature where their bodies met rose several degrees. Lee clutched at his back, need building deep inside of her.

After another mystery move with his lips, she opened to him. He dipped his tongue in, meeting hers in a warm, sensual tangle. Then he pulled back.

Waited to see if she wanted more.

Oh yes, more.

Lee leaned against him and swept her tongue against his partly open mouth. The embrace deepened as he surrounded her with his frame. Little lights sparkled at the edge of her vision. Her toes tingled. Her legs went weak. Still, he held her steady, taking his time, meeting her kiss for kiss, there in the doctors' lounge.

A *bang* in the hallway followed by a squeak caught her attention. Jumping, she glanced back over her shoulder. He tightened his arms around her. Another softer squeak came from the hall.

"What was that?" she said, breathless like she'd run a marathon.

Maverick cocked his head to listen. "Environmental services cart going by."

Lee dropped her forehead on his chest. "Mood busted by a mop."

Maverick rested his chin on the top of her head, and his chuckle vibrated through her skull. "As much fun as that was, this is probably not the right place. Contrary to what the popular television shows might suggest."

It wasn't right for lots of reasons. This place, this situation. Her life. Lee had emotional baggage to unpack. Financial hills to climb. Never in the past had she taken relationships lightly. This assignment was temporary. Best she remember that fact.

All her brain remembered was the sensation of Maverick's warm mouth sweeping over hers while he sheltered her in his embrace. She scrunched her toes in her shoes and rolled her lips together, tasting him on her skin. Hells bells, she needed to pull herself together.

"That was ..." he began.

"A heck of a support hug?"

He slid his hand from the back of her head to rest on her shoulder. "Yeah. That."

"Do you support the rest of your EMS team this way?" Shifting weight from one foot to the other, she brushed against him and groaned at the faint friction of her chest against his.

He bent down for a simple, soft kiss, heaved out a massive lungful of air, then let go of her and backed up. One step. Then two. Her skin cooled even as she involuntarily leaned forward.

"Supporting the EMS team like this?" his voice cracked as his gaze never left hers. "Moose's wife would not be impressed with my staff management skills. Do you know how quickly I'd be written up?"

Dropping her hands to her sides, she added some physical space between them. Her face burned and nerves still tingled, but she peeked up at him. It had been so long since she'd enjoyed such sensations.

Truly had never felt like this if Lee was being completely honest with herself. "Well. Okay, then." What did someone say in this situation? "Thanks?" Lee closed her eyes. That wasn't the right word.

"Hey," he said.

Peeking through one eye, she spied his sheepish smile. A safe reaction. Lee could deal with a little adult embarrassment. She rubbed sweaty palms on her pants.

"So." He pointed with both index fingers. "I'm going to head on out."

"Have a good night."

A gusting *whoosh* was accompanied by the rise and fall of his chest. "Not a problem after that kiss."

Her cheeks heated again as she bent to pick up the napkins and snack packaging, wadding them up in a tighter and tighter ball, like she wanted to compress the awkwardness.

"At the risk of sounding too forward," Mav said in a serious tone of voice, "any interest in having that dinner?"

"Now?" She squeaked the word.

"No, in the next few days."

Her thoughts whirled, but her mind was clearer than it had been in a long time.

How could this connection feel both too fast and too slow? She didn't care. She wanted to experience more of it.

"Sure," she managed.

He nodded. "Then I'll also let you see my babies."

"Babies?" Oh, he had children? Okay.

Maverick winked and strode toward the lounge door. "I'll line up our call schedules and we'll find a time that works."

Chapter Ten

ON TUESDAY THE next week, Lee slid her cafeteria tray down the line as the food service workers chatted and dished up lunch. Today's special was Dungeness crab and wild mushroom chowder with a piece of fresh sourdough bread. Lee's mouth watered as she inhaled the fresh aromas and swiped her employee badge at the cash register.

Thank God her meals were covered by the hospital. Lee's credit card would barely make it to this Friday's first paycheck. At least her new booties had arrived to replace the ones ruined in the snow. She wiggled her toes. Comfortable.

Pricey, though not as expensive as the Gianni Bini booties. See? Getting an off brand saved money. Not that anyone at the hospital would care if she showed up in tennis shoes and scrubs each day, as long as she took great care of patients.

Lee stood up straighter. It was important to project professionalism, which definitely included her attire. At some point, her salary would catch up with her debt load, and she'd be back on an even financial keel.

Until then, she would stick with free cafeteria food and discount shoes.

The hospital cafeteria had four-person tables in the center of the room as well as a line of smaller tables along one windowed wall, which was where she sat. Pushing up her maroon sweater sleeves, she picked up the spoon. At the first bite of tender crab in creamy broth with a mushroom piece flavored by thyme and shallot, she leaned back and hummed in happiness. Her eyes drifted closed as she chewed. The flavor and textures of the first bite—she'd never had anything quite like this before. The local foods tasted nothing like the down-home Southern food she was accustomed to eating.

A deep chuckle made her open one eye. "Are you open to company, or is this more of a private moment?" Maverick hovered a few feet away, holding a tray full of food. His navy EMS coat highlighted his broad shoulders.

Warmth climbed Lee's neck. A peek at his mouth sent a flash of memory. Maverick's arms around her and his lips nipping, tasting, opening her to his kisses. She shifted in the seat.

Then her stomach rumbled, and she caved to a different temptation. "You're welcome to join me."

He draped his coat on the chair behind him, sat across from her, and swiped off his beanie, running his hand through his light brown hair.

Lee's fingers itched to smooth the tousled waves.

Then Maverick picked up a spoon and inhaled, followed by an eye-rolling, blissed-out first bite of the chowder. "Amazing as always. Chef Yuka is a genius."

"I'll say." She took another spoonful then broke off a corner of fresh sourdough, dipping it in the chowder, and chewing in happiness as the tang of the dough mixed with the crab and flavorings.

With a shiver, she peered out the window at the snow swirling over the pine-dotted hills behind the hospital. Today's weather included cold haze and meager sunshine for a few hours. Chowder was a perfect meal.

After a few minutes of eating in companionable silence, Maverick cleared his throat as his brows drew together.

Uh-oh.

He set down the spoon. "Sorry about bailing on Monday night's dinner plan. Hilda's son got sick, so I took her shift."

Lee could appreciate unpredictable schedules when plans had to change.

Her ex? Not so much. Preston yelled at her if she missed a social function or was late to a business event because of a delivery. In fact, patient care flat-out pissed him off, because it meant during those times, Preston Dupree wasn't her priority.

He never understood why she couldn't call in sick when he had a social engagement or if he needed a spouse to join golfing couples, where he spent his time ignoring her as he schmoozed his way up the local government ladder.

How much had he spent on their country club memberships?

More than she had spent on state licensing and professional organization membership.

Criminelly, she hated schmoozing, and she didn't like to golf, much less do those things together.

Almost as much as she hated—

"Penny for your thoughts?" Maverick's low voice and brush of his fingers over her wrist pulled her back. "You can verify my shift log if you don't believe me."

"What? Monday night? Oh gosh no, I believe you."

"You sure? For a minute there you looked mad. Dee says that I should start most conversations with an apology, just in case." His brows drew together. "This may be one of those times. If I said something wrong yet again, my bad."

Lee stared at the spoon lying next to the half-eaten chowder bowl, her stomach tightening. *Quit it.* Maverick was *not* Preston. "I know how coverage changes quickly in a rural area like this. At some point, I'll be the one changing plans." Assuming there were future plans. "I was thinking about other things, is all."

"Like how to disembowel someone but not leave any evidence?"

Hoo boy. "You're not far off!" Lee said as she relaxed and dug back into her lunch. Delicious.

His jaw dropped. "Wait. What?"

"What?" She chewed and swallowed. "I haven't disemboweled anyone that you would be aware of." She tapped her napkin to her mouth and grinned at his brow-furrowed expression. "Wonderful lunch!"

"Uh-huh," he mumbled with his head tilted to one side. He lifted his glass and gulped some water.

She tapped her index finger on the table. "Hold on. This doesn't count as credit for dinner, does it?"

With a scrape of metal on crockery, Maverick polished off his meal and patted his firm midsection with a contented growl that she responded to in ways that weren't appropriate in a hospital cafeteria. "No, this is not dinner date. This is lunch with a fellow hospital employee on chowder day." He lifted his chin toward his partner, who was chatting with two friends at one of the larger tables. "Louise always knows when it's chowder day at the Yukon Valley Hospital cafeteria."

Lee laughed. "Oh, so my pleasant company secondary to your hunger?"

He leaned forward, voice quiet so only Lee could hear. "Chowder hunger versus pleasant company hunger are two very different things. I'm lucky to be enjoying both right now, but I have only satisfied my chowder hunger." He rested his blunt fingertips on top of hers—the tiniest heated contact—and pinned her with an intense stare. "At some point, I'd like to have seconds of the pleasant company."

"I—" An involuntary shudder worked its way through her torso.

Maverick's demeanor crumbled as he flashed a self-deprecating grimace. "You'll notice my expert use of crab chowder as a flirtation device." He dropped his forehead against his palm. "I know. Real suave."

Covering her mouth to contain the laugh erupting, she finally composed herself, but not before other staff glanced her way. She smoothed her sweater hem and murmured, "Ranks right up there with a Code Blue as a prelude to a kiss."

"Hey, that was happenstance. Also, I like the way you think. We should come up with another emergency." He nodded with a gleam in his blue eyes that made her toes tingle. "But to fully answer your question, my point is, I'm not trying to get out of dinner. We can shoot for this Thursday? A little after seven at the diner?"

"Works for me."

He opened his mouth to say something, but a beeping noise stopped him. Pulling out his phone, he lifted his hand in a wave. Louise gave a thumbs-up in response and grabbed her tray, getting up from her table.

"Gotta go, Lee." Maverick pressed his palm down on the back of her hand where it rested on the table. "See you for dinner in a few days, barring any natural disasters or acts of God."

THAT FRIDAY, LEE woke up at six a.m. before work and breathlessly logged onto her Georgia bank's website. She squinted at the screen's brightness, harsh in the morning darkness. The dinner date with Mav *in a few days* hadn't happened due to her schedule. Probably for the best. If they had split the bill, she might have been in trouble.

Shivering, she snagged the light blue throw blanket off of the functional but worn couch in the living room and wrapped it around her flannel-pajama-clad frame as she settled in the chair at the small dinette table. Drumming her fingers on the tabletop, she waited. Speeds might be slow, but thanks to rural broadband, at least she had internet out here.

Come on, she urged the screen.

One of the clinic nurses was having a baby shower next week. When the envelope to add gift money had come across Lee's desk yesterday, she had wanted to contribute but instead pretended she'd left her wallet at home. Hot shame had churned in her stomach afterward.

She was literally down to her last dollar.

Damn Preston, her life, those lawyers. All of it. She clutched the blanket.

Her credit card payments were due by tomorrow. Even though her student loans were in temporary forbearance, it was important to restart monthly payments ASAP before the accrued interest blew the roof off of the balance.

The bank's website loaded. She clicked on the link to her account.

Blinked.

Looked again. Her heart pounded as she searched the screen.

There were funds now present, but not as much as she had anticipated. She needed more than that to make a dent in her balances. What happened? Sweat broke out on her upper lip.

She checked once more. The amount deposited was around half of what she had planned for.

Air sawed in and out of her lungs. *What?*

Switching tabs, she pulled up the locums company employee portal on her computer and double-checked that she had submitted her hours correctly. Yes, she had submitted two weeks' worth of work. However, she had only gotten paid for one week, because—

Biweekly payments.

Damn. It. To. Hell.

Lee had only been paid for her first week of locums because the second week would get paid in two weeks and—oh, she crammed shaking fingers through her tangled hair.

Her eyes burned. Gut ached.

Nowhere in medical school or residency was she given education about finances, other than an attending physician recommending that the residents get a good financial planner to manage their money. No discussion of how to work through the staggering debt medical students took on. No classes on how to set up a budget on the modest resident salary, especially when one's spouse wanted to spend money like she was an attending physician already. That was the first step into the hole right there.

A laugh turned into a sob. No planner would take her on as a client now. She had no money! Lee stared blankly at the white walls of the empty kitchen and living room decorated with a few generic neutral prints. No one sat across from her at the bare table. Down the street a truck engine rumbled to life as someone warmed up their vehicle. Off in the distance, she detected the high whine of a snowmobile running at speed. Someone's early morning commute.

What was she doing with her life? What was she doing *here*? It would feel so good to unburden herself and share her shame. She had quite the collection of mistakes. She swallowed. No. The Tiptons never, *ever* let on about financial struggles. She looked around again at the empty room until her eyes landed on the new leather booties near the front door.

They *were* super cute, even if they were Bini knockoffs.

Successful people found a way to appear successful.

Thanks, Mom. Super helpful.

This entire situation was not what she had envisioned for her career, working for the highest bidder. Coldest place on Earth, in a neat but modest rental house in a tiny town, alone and buried under mountains of debt, unable to let on that she felt like a fraud because everyone thought if she was a doctor she must be successful.

Not every doctor had an ex-husband who had taken everything.

Not every doctor had gotten buried by credit card debt like she had.

How long would it be before she trusted herself again?

Not even her pride remained, and that stung the most.

Blinking back tears, she sniffled and logged onto the credit card sites.

Two maxed out cards with credit limits set way too high.

She clicked. Two minimum payments made.

Two more weeks until her bank account would contain money again.

Lee tucked her legs up under her, pulled the quilt more tightly around her, and sat alone in the rental, trapped in Yukon Valley.

Chapter Eleven

A S IT TURNED out, lining up two different call schedules for people with two different types of healthcare occupations, in a resource-strapped environment like Yukon Valley where emergencies upended everyone's day, challenged even Mav's matrix schedule design skills. Another week had passed.

Here it was, Friday midday, and he'd completed preparations for the guests coming in later today for the weekend. Hell, as of today, it was now February.

In no time it would be March.

And because Dee told him the initial length of Lee's locums assignment, he also knew what came after March.

Nothing.

He and Lee hadn't managed to do more than have lunch together in the cafeteria a few times. While he enjoyed her company, he could sense the professional walls she kept around her while in the hospital. Frankly, he tried to do the same. Didn't matter that he knew every employee by first name—he and Lee were in a workplace. He still needed to maintain decorum, even if decorum was the last thing on his mind when her tongue flicked over her lower lip, or her cheeks turned pink when he stared at her too long.

Last week's anticipated date hadn't materialized because Lee had to rush in and help Dr. Burmeister with an urgent C-section that evening. Something about breech twins at thirty-three weeks gestational age. Mav thanked his lucky stars he didn't have to professionally deal with that situation as an EMT. Those little babies had gone to Fairbanks with the NICU team that had flown in on a fixed-wing to transport them.

Those newborns in no way respected Lee's schedule. The stinkers.

Tomorrow, though. She would meet him here at the house for a tour of the property and to see his babies. Might stay for an hour or so. If the day went well, they might go out for dinner later or have a meal at the house. No structured plans. Casual. No pressure.

A thump under his ribs and sweaty palms told a different story. He straightened up pictures on the mantel for the tenth time this morning. Truth be told, the tidying up wasn't for the guests' benefit.

He had taken time to tame his unruly hair—normally, it lived in chaos under the beanie. He hadn't had time to get it cut, but at least with a little hair gel he wouldn't look like that Grizzly Adams character. He'd also carefully shaved this morning, not rushing like his usual slice-and-dice routine. He would repeat the effort tomorrow morning before Lee arrived.

Glancing down, he patted his navy flannel shirt tucked neatly into his coated, insulated cargo pants. Guest arrival day meant he needed presentable but functional clothing.

He glanced over at Kenai, who lounged half asleep on her back near the great room fireplace, her tongue lolling to one side. Hopefully, she'd continue relaxing, along with the other dogs happily tucked in their kennels out back.

Scooping up the latest bills from yesterday's trip to the post office box, he saw two red past-due stamps and shook his head. Another envelope was from the Bureau of Land Management—at least it didn't appear to be a bill. Lastly, a large manila envelope had a US Geologic Survey return address. Again, not a bill, so not something he would deal with right now. Mav had no idea why BLM or USGS wanted anything to do with him. He and Dee held land and mineral rights to the property, not that there was anything worth digging up. He shoved the letters and two bills into the top kitchen desk drawer, adding to the thick pile already there.

Later.

For now, he wanted to think about a certain woman from Georgia who had felt perfect in his arms. Those lips. Man, she could kiss. Her body fit against his like a puzzle piece. It had taken a superhuman effort for him to walk away in the doctors' lounge last week. He tugged at his pants and swallowed. Hopefully, he could keep a level head and concentrate on a visit—and only a friendly visit—tomorrow.

Didn't matter if he hoped one thing would lead to an-other—her time here was limited. Anything serious wouldn't work, and Mav wouldn't risk another wilderness relationship disaster. No, he'd enjoy friendship with Lee and show her his dogs and the beauty of the tundra. That was it.

The sour flavor on his tongue tasted like disappointed resolve.

A message popped up on his phone, relayed to him via the house's satellite Wi-Fi, not through a cell tower. Living several miles away from town there weren't any towers close enough for a signal.

Lee wrote, *T-minus one day until I get to see the babies!*

Mav had explained early on that his babies were indeed sled dogs, in case she thought he had random small children hanging around. He replied, *Can't wait. It'll be a fun day.* Unless the predicted storm kicked up. Then it would be a miserable day.

Hopefully, she had good gear.

Hopefully, the guests also had proper gear and solid knowledge of operating a "snowgo," as Dad liked to call the snowmachines. Mav had tuned up their fleet of six sleds, accumulated over time by his parents and kept on hand for guests' use. All running smoothly, as of this morning.

Bring warm clothing, he replied.

Will stop by Three Bears to pick up a few things. I'll figure out what all I need when I get to your place. Followed by a snowman emoji and a hands-up shrug emoji.

He grinned like a college kid messaging a crush.

Nope. Friends. That was it.

Besides, he had work to do.

With the guests arriving this afternoon, he had taken several days off EMS duties so that he could play host.

Although Mav didn't like the idea of double dipping— going on a date while technically hosting guests—it was the best option they could line up for now. Lee at least understood unpredictability and didn't seem to get mad when plans changed.

Also, it wasn't a date, damn it.

Over the past week, they had texted regularly. At first, the texts involved shuffling their dinner date timing, then they basically gave up on schedule coordination. Somehow the messages morphed into random funny observations throughout the day and a few almost-flirty texts in the evening.

Mav never thought the sight of a red dot on his phone messages icon could make him smile. The first time it had happened, he stopped what he was doing and stared at the display. Louise called him out for the goofy grin on his face.

Busted.

A day ago, Dee had leaned into him again, probing for info on his relationship.

What relationship? There was no time.

Instead, Mav used what little free time he had this past week to work extra EMS shifts in anticipation of time off and to prepare for his guests. If he wanted to make this place an all-season wilderness retreat destination, then he needed to impress visitors. He gave the babies lots of attention and let them haul him through the snowy tundra on several yappy, snow-eating hikes and even had them pull the sled over a few miles of trail. Anything to make up for this upcoming weekend's planned lack of activity.

He had stocked enough groceries to cook meals for a small army. Using his small off-road ute with the plow attachment, he'd cleared paths on the property and bladed his long gravel driveway multiple times. Each time another few inches fell, he replowed. No way would his guests get stuck before they reached the front door. The business needed good reviews, word of mouth, and repeat customers, or he risked losing the family lodge.

He glared at the kitchen desk drawer holding the collections letters. Failure was not an option.

Over in the great room, Kenai lifted her head. A minute later, the sound of a vehicle pulling up outside reached Mav. He glanced at the clock.

Guests were three hours early.

Car doors closed.

Nothing to do but be a good host.

Chapter Twelve

LATE SATURDAY MORNING, Lee peered through the windshield at the clear blue sky. There was an actual sun low but visible above the hills. Sunrise now occurred around nine thirty a.m. She'd been here only three weeks and had grown accustomed to the late twilight dawn and early dusk. Now it surprised her how she could feel the difference in an extra hour of daylight as she left January behind.

Five miles west of town, she watched for the righthand turn off the lightly traveled state highway that would take her to Maverick's lodge. She had Googled his business, and the website's pictures showed the beautiful surrounding area in various seasons. Wiggling her toasty fingers in the glove liners with Gore-Tex mittens on top, thanks to Maverick's recommendation, she took a breath in and out, trying to slow her pattering heartbeat.

She shifted in the seat. The layers of fleece underneath her snow pants made the backs of her knees sweat.

Maverick had said to bring good gear for cold weather.

The shopping spree at Three Bears had been financially and fashionably ambitious. Unfortunately, now she wore all of it. Lee tugged at her neckline, letting some air pass between insulative thermal shirts, a vest, and a zipped jacket.

So warm. Rookie mistake.

At the temperature readout on the dashboard, she shook her head. Minus ten outside but a tropical sauna in her polar expedition outfit. *Welp, learn a new lesson every day.*

She glanced at the paper map he had left for her in an envelope in the doctors' lounge. That was what their communication had boiled down to—notes left at drop locations. And silly, random texts.

Right before she turned, a large maroon SUV peeled out of the side road and fishtailed onto the highway, the engine revving as it barely missed hitting her car.

Lee yelped and stomped the brakes but immediately eased off the pedal, somehow remembering that sudden stops increased the likelihood of wrecking on a snowy road. Thankfully, no one traveled on the road behind her, or she'd have been rear-ended.

Crawling to a stop, she sat, unable to move, hands still gripping the wheel, heart thumping against her ribs. What the heck?

Another peek in the rearview mirror—the SUV had nearly disappeared. Lee flicked the turn signal with a shaking hand and eased her sedan onto the plowed gravel dirt road that led to Mav's home. Next to the narrow drive, towers of snow rose higher than her vehicle's roof.

After a few hundred feet, leafless trees and dark green spruces rose on either side of the drive, creating a cocoon out of the wilderness. The state highway was only a short distance behind her, but as she wound around gentle switchbacks that seemed fitted around the stands of trees, it felt like she traveled to the very end of the Earth.

A few more minutes of carefully navigating up and over a hillside, then the road finally leveled into an open parking area.

As she pulled up near to what looked like the front door, she leaned forward and peered out. "Wow."

A massive rustic log home appeared as if it rose from the forest. It was surrounded by snow-covered trees. A steep roof with frozen icicles off metal eaves capped a covered front entrance that projected out to a small porch with three stairs leading to the ground. She identified the feature as a typical Arctic entry that held boots and coats before opening into the rest of the main house. The two-story lodge—more like a lodge than a simple house—had a one-story section added to the right side of the structure, only half-visible due to the feet of snow on the ground.

She parked and opened her door, snagging her backpack that contained even more winter gear. With this many layers on, the cold didn't touch her.

Wind gusted over her. *Brr.* Except for her exposed face.

Frantic yaps rose from behind the house. The babies.

Off to the left of the lodge stood three small cabins, their roofs barely visible with the snow all around. A clear path was plowed to the first cabin's porch. Six snowmobiles with covers on them were parked nearby.

She glimpsed distant mountains, partially visible through breaks in the stands of trees next to the lodge. Crisp, fresh air with a hint of woodsmoke enticed her to inhale again. Back in northeast Georgia, she had vacationed in a rental cabin that was tucked in the picturesque southern Appalachian mountains, but she'd never experienced a remote, stark, and beautiful setting like this one.

The front door opened, and Maverick stepped out. He wore a pine-green-and-black-checked button-down shirt with leather patches on the shoulders. The shirt tucked into dark gray pants that hugged his hips and muscled thighs with rugged perfection. The thick boots he wore were halfway unlaced and loose at the calf, like he'd quickly pulled them on to greet her. He leaned against the doorframe, like he was a part of the Alaskan scenery.

"You found it." His low voice cut through the cold morning like a clear bell.

"Almost didn't survive the trip." She closed the door and tromped in her new insulated boots on the snow-packed gravel.

Stopping at the foot of the three steps, she looked up. Maverick stood, feet shoulder width apart, like a hardy mountain man in his domain and utterly unfazed by the subzero temperatures.

He extended his bare hand to help her ascend the steps. She stopped on the small square entry porch, and he released the firm grasp.

"Can I take your bag?" he asked.

She handed it to him. "Sure."

"What happened that you almost didn't make it here?"

"An SUV just about ran me over coming out of this driveway. Were those the guests?"

"Damn it." A scowl marred his appearance as a congenial

host. "Sorry."

"Yikes. Well, they must be enjoying their stay."

"A little too much." He ran a hand over surprisingly tame hair and shrugged. "Come on in." A wary, uneasy expression furrowed his brow as he looked at the entry then back to Lee.

As though he worried what she would think.

Lee stepped into the entry and sat on the bench to tug off her boots and hang her coat. Thick, quick *clacks* and a *whuff* preceded two paws on her knee with a small wolfish head studying her.

"Oh, hi there, honey." She smiled. The dog had gray around the muzzle, brown eyes that gazed up at her, and a wildly whipping tail. Short, scruffy hair covered her head, but that tail was a waving flag of long fluff.

"Kenai, down, girl." The dog reluctantly complied with a baleful expression toward Maverick.

"It's okay." Lee took off her mittens and glove liners and set them on the bench. She gave the dog the back of her hand to sniff. After receiving an approving lick, Lee scratched behind the dog's ears and jowls and crooned, "You're a pretty one, Kenai." The dog put her paws right back up on Lee's leg and huffed. "My goodness, so friendly."

"Not to everyone. Usually she's shy around strangers." He gestured. "This is different for her."

"Seems perfectly social to me." Lee gave several solid pats against Kenai's flank. "Wow, she's solid."

"Kenai is a keeper. Also, she's middle-aged."

Lee tilted her head up. "What's that mean?"

"A keeper means that she can eat two kibbles and still gain weight." He grinned. "As for her normal attitude, I would call her standoffishly able to tolerate other humans, but not *affectionate*."

Lee cupped the dog's head and gazed into the soulful brown eyes. "Girl, same. I identify with all of you."

Maverick chuckled and cupped an elbow to help Lee stand. He studied her, paused, started to smile, then pressed his lips together. His blue eyes twinkled.

"What?" she said.

He shook his head.

Lee patted her dense clothing. "What? Too much?"

"How are you not roasting in all of that?"

She looked down at the bunched-up rolls of insulated layers upon layers. It *was* a little difficult to move. "I might look like a marshmallow, but I'm warm." Wiping her damp brow, she said, "Fine. You're right. It's too much clothing. I didn't know what to wear. If we're not going out right away, I might peel off a few layers." Lee unzipped the polar fleece jacket and shrugged it off.

"Need help?"

She whipped her head around.

A tilt of his chin and rueful expression warmed her more than snuggling into a thick coat. "With balancing." He grinned. "While you peel."

"*Hmmph.*" After a few more hops and shimmies and Maverick's solid supporting arm, Lee made it down to the base layer of thick fleece leggings, a Capilene long-sleeve top, a lightweight synthetic vest, and wool socks.

Maverick's blue gaze swept over her, narrowing as his scrutiny drifted down to her legs. She wasn't indecent. Heck, she was more clothed than her mom's Lululemon-clad friends brunching after Pilates class.

That flash of desire in his eyes triggered a heat building low in her abdomen that had nothing to do with being overdressed.

Actually, it had everything to do with being overdressed. *Shoo wee.*

Quit it. What her ovaries wanted, what her temporary situation necessitated, and what her heart could handle were three very different things.

What if her situation became permanent? The minute that thought hit her brain she squashed it. Yukon Valley was a financial means to an end, plain and simple. And a temporary one at that.

"Come on, then. I'll give you the grand tour." He motioned for her to precede him.

Lee and Kenai followed.

Chapter Thirteen

M AV WATCHED LEE'S reaction as they strolled into the great room. Damn it, but her opinion mattered, more than he wanted to admit.

He tried to view the lodge through her eyes, but all he could see were past memories and current issues. He pictured Christmastime with Mom and Dad and with Dee and her husband from years ago, all sitting on the couches and recliners, enjoying a brightly lit tree, the warm fire, and comfortable conversation. A pinch in his chest refocused his attention to the brown and blue patterned rug between two couches. The once-thick fabric had become worn, frayed on one edge. One of the west-facing windows had fogged, its seal broken. Needed to be replaced. On the back corner of the great room, a river rock stone had fallen out of the mortar of the fireplace and Mav hadn't had time to reset it.

That hollow space in the stonework resonated in more ways than one.

Lee hadn't said anything. He didn't need her to be impressed, just accepting.

"Wow," she breathed, her head tilted back to take in the high ceiling and hand-carved wood railing of the loft above them.

That one word resuscitated Mav's hope.

She walked straight ahead to the soaring windows on the side of the fireplace, Kenai sedately tagging along. Lee lifted her hand but didn't quite touch the glass. "This view is amazing. The meadow, the woods behind it, and those mountains. Gosh." As if to herself, she said, "It's so pretty, it doesn't seem real."

He rocked back on his heels. Why didn't he think she would appreciate it?

Because he had automatically lumped her in with Skylar, whose first comments upon entering the lodge included how cold it was and how slow the satellite Wi-Fi ran.

Quit comparing. He did Lee a disservice. He did his older, wiser self a disservice.

He loved this place. He would work himself into the ground to keep it in the family. He needed to make it successful, but without time or money … Frowning at an area of unvarnished wood on the windowsill, he added another item to his mental to-do list.

"What do you think?" His voice came out hoarse. "I know it's not very fancy." He had said those same words before. Mav braced himself.

He couldn't see her full expression, only her lovely profile as she studied the scenery. He stepped back behind her, wanting to touch her but rolling his hands into fists and planting them at his sides. He peered over her head to visualize what she saw when she stared out this window.

"Fancy? This is very Alaska rustic chic, like on the TV shows! Honestly, no one I know would believe a place like this exists." She gave a mirthless laugh. "No one I know would survive it!"

He knew all about outsiders not surviving here. "How so?"

"Besides the fact that it's so beautiful it almost hurts?"

Mav knew all about something being so beautiful it almost hurt.

He was looking at her. "Yes."

"First of all, there are no boutique shops in town for Mom. No malls for hundreds of miles. Even if she bought jewelry or fancy clothes to show off, they would be wasted under the winter coats. On the other hand, Dad is lost without a country club to attend. The lack of year-round blooming greenery would shock them to their socks. No golfing and drinks afterward with buddies who helped my ex—" She bit off the last word and fell silent.

Maverick didn't move. He wanted to know more but wouldn't press.

"Anyway." She pressed a fingertip into the casement. "My family thinks I've lost my mind with this job and location."

"Do you think you've lost your mind by coming here?" He caught a whiff of her sweet and tart scent that reminded him of salmonberries baked in a pie.

It took a few seconds for her to say anything. The words were so soft he barely heard them.

"Maybe so. Or maybe the exact opposite."

"How so?"

"I really needed this job," she said heatedly but didn't go

into details. Her sigh slid over him like silk on raw nerves. "I'm realizing that *home* might not be one fixed place or one group of people. *Home* doesn't equal *welcoming*, either." She also did not elaborate on that statement.

He definitely wanted to know the whole story of why her shoulders slumped.

Kenai took that moment to lift her head into Lee's hand, insisting on another ear scratch. With a chuckle, Lee obliged.

The quiet moment dissolved like rising morning mist.

Clearing his throat, he said, "Want to see more?"

When she turned, Lee bumped into him, and he instinctively grasped her upper arm. As she tilted her head up, she caught her lower lip beneath her teeth. That small action, combined with a hint of sadness in her brown eyes, fired off a cascade of complex sensations wrapped up in Mav's own conflicted feelings and topped off with tons of his baggage from the past.

The mere mention of her ex had created creases between her brows and made her beautiful mouth turn downward. Mav needed to know what happened, if only to be better than whatever *that* guy was.

Hell. He'd made at least three inappropriate assumptions in the past minute, most of which involved a future, which Mav and Lee did not have.

Not a good way to start a visit—he peered down at her open, vulnerable expression—with a friend.

Friend, damn it.

He dropped his hand. "Come on, this way. We'll check out the main floor bedroom, the loft rooms, and then the guest wing."

She blinked, and pain was replaced by a polite smile.

He recognized a mask when he saw one.

"The guest wing must be fancy!" she said.

It wasn't for him to press. He would remain sensitive to her privacy and keep things casual and friendly. Patience wasn't his strongest talent, but if she wanted to open up to him, she could do so on her terms. "It only sounds fancy."

Kenai, apparently not interested in the grand tour, licked Lee's hand one more time, padded over to the foam bed in front of the fireplace, and curled up with a satisfied *whuff.*

Chapter Fourteen

AFTER THE INTERIOR lodge tour followed by a light lunch, Lee and Maverick cleaned up the dishes together. For such a mundane activity, it felt personal. Intimate. He handed her another plate to dry, and their fingers brushed. When she reached to open a cabinet, their hips bumped, each small contact making her skin tingle.

For a space of time, she wasn't a doctor, and he wasn't a paramedic. They didn't live four thousand miles apart. She didn't have self-doubt and massive debt weighing on her. They were just two people hanging out together. No social pressures. No impending work emergencies. No relationship issues. No drama.

A little drama with Maverick could be fun. She scanned the great room. Kisses by the fire. Talking about hobbies and dreams. Meals and laughter shared. More kisses.

His warm voice broke her out of those wispy thoughts. "Want to head out and meet the rest of the crew?"

"Sounds good. Do I need all my layers?"

He dried his hands on a towel and reached up to tuck a stray piece of hair behind her ear. They both froze for a half second.

His eyelids lowered. "Layers?" With a blink, he dropped

his hand. Then Maverick's laugh brushed past her like snow on a breeze. "No. You only need about half of what you brought." He pointed to the thermometer mounted outside of the kitchen window with a digital display on the window-sill. "We'll be active, and temp's up to zero."

"Yay?" Still sounded cold.

"I'm happy with anything in positive digits during winter here. There's a big difference between minus forty and zero."

Lee had no frame of reference, other than both tempera-tures seemed unpleasant.

They donned the appropriate clothing and exited through the front door, followed by Kenai. Heading toward the side of the lodge, their boots squeaked along a path of packed, dry snow. Clouds had moved in over the past hour.

Maverick wore what looked like a rock-climbing type of harness that wrapped around his hips and upper thighs, with a loop in the front to clip the dogs' leashes. Lee swallowed. Those snug straps emphasized his ... winter landscape. Wow. She stumbled on uneven snow. If Lee didn't pay attention, she'd end up face-first in a drift. Dressed in her pink doggie harness, Kenai yapped as she eagerly pulled against the leash Lee held in her hand.

"For a medium-sized dog, she's strong!" Lee said from behind him.

"She's excited to be going for a walk with a new person." Maverick stopped and turned back with a quirk to his mouth. "Sure you don't need me to take her?"

"No, I'm fine. It's quite an experience."

"First timers are always surprised by the dogs' power.

Good sled dogs aren't puffy giant huskies, like people think. For distance racing, it's best if they're in the thirty- to sixty-pound range and lean. Smaller dogs mean less food weight to carry on the sled." He pointed. "They love to pull anything. Kenai here has been my lead dog for many years. Great nose for the trail. Keeps the other dogs in line."

Kenai strained against the harness, dragging Lee forward. "What kind of dog is she?"

"Technically Alaskan husky, but that breed is a blend of different types of Nordic dogs. They're designed to have the strength, personality, and desire to pull sleds." He paused and studied Kenai, who paused and stared up at him with her tongue hanging out. "They're not considered pretty dogs."

"I disagree with that statement!" Fine, Kenai was scruffy and off-balance with her fluffy tail and scraggly mud-colored hair on her head. The sweet doggy grin made her cute. "Do they still pull sleds?"

He continued along the path. "We don't race anymore. Almost every day, I get them out for walks in the woods, though they still prefer to run with a sled attached. On those days, I hitch up a cart in the summer or a sled in the winter, and off we go!"

As they reached the far side of the clearing behind the house, the yapping and howls increased. Four dogs, each one jumping against their staked leads or perched on top of their kennel roofs, barked as she and Maverick approached. Kenai answered with a hoarse yapping howl of her own, then looked back, as if to make sure it was okay to make noise.

"Don't they get cold?" Lee shouted over the cacophony.

"I check on them regularly in frigid temps, but they enjoy wintry weather. Also, I keep fresh straw bedding in each kennel, so they can get out of the elements if need be." His care for the dogs was obvious. "If it truly is too cold, I can bring them into the garage or even the house."

"Like Kenai?"

"As she aged, it became clear she didn't tolerate being outdoors for long periods of time, so she mostly stays inside during winter."

"They're all retired?"

"I don't race anymore." That wasn't the answer to her question. Interesting.

"You only have five dogs? On TV, it seems like there are lots more running races." She eyed several other empty kennels.

"Any number of dogs can pull a sled. It has more to do with the weight of the sled and musher, the distance, the terrain, and the purpose of the activity. Recreational rides on groomed trails are fine with two or three dogs. Long-distance racers run teams of twelve to fourteen, dropping any injured or tired dogs at checkpoints. For the Iditarod, you only have to have five dogs on the string when you finish the race in Nome." He patted the head of the nearest dog whose tongue lolled out of one corner of its mouth as it stood on back legs to greet Maverick. "I kept my oldest dogs and gave the younger ones to friends who still race." Gesturing down at the nearest dog who had a white and black fur pattern, he shot her a big grin. "Want to meet everyone?"

Her heart warmed. "You bet!"

"This here fellow is Klister. Runs next to Kenai in lead or behind her in swing position. Will do anything to avoid me putting booties on him." He slipped the dog into a harness and got him to hold still long enough to put on red nylon booties.

Lee petted Klister and followed Maverick.

"This lovely girl is Denali."

"She looks different than the others." Lee took her mitten and glove liner off to sink her fingers into the fuzzy light brown fur over the dog's otherwise white face. The dog's eye color was a shocking ice blue, almost white.

"Yes, she's a malamute. They're generally fluffier. She is great at the wheel position."

"Wheel?"

"Closest to the sled. Pulls all day long, any weight, any distance." He moved over another several feet. "This goofball is Bob. He's what happens if you took spare parts and crammed them together to make another dog. Not much to look at, but he knows how to pull at the wheel position."

Bob had an adorable overbite, different colored legs, one ear that stood up while the other one flopped down, and a deep blue eye paired with a light brown eye. Somehow, too, his shoulders weren't proportional to his hips. "Oh, he's pitiful, bless his heart."

Bob nosed the bare hand she offered and licked it, *whuffing* his doggy approval as Maverick slid the harness and booties on him.

Finally, they reached the last dog, a larger sturdy black

and gray dog whose whipping tail made his whole butt wiggle from side to side. Lee studied his slightly cross-eyed expression. He seemed … simple but happy.

"And this is Kaaktuq."

"That's an interesting name."

"In Inuit, it roughly translates to *hungry*, which is the perpetual state he's in. He'll eat anything, even if it's not edible." As the dog leapt up, Maverick held his paws up to his midsection and slipped on booties. "Right, buddy? You like keeping our local veterinarian in business. In other medical mysteries, his flatulence is remarkable, which I know firsthand because guess where it blows?" At the innocent, blank expression on the dog's face, Maverick leaned over to Lee and whispered, "Kaaktuq here is also dumber than two rocks smashed together."

Lee shivered at his low voice so close to her ear, and then burst out laughing. "It can't be that bad."

"The gas or the brains?" Maverick grinned. "Listen. It's good he's a team dog and doesn't have to make any decisions. Hitch him up and let him run. He'd go forever if I didn't make him take a break now and then." He bent and covered the dog's ears. "Between you and me, Kaaktuq couldn't navigate his way out of an empty box. Shh, don't tell him."

"Poor guy." Her stomach hurt from laughing at all of the characters.

After Maverick placed the harness, Kaaktuq licked him again and then sat down, tail still wagging, making an arc in the snow. He followed Maverick's every action with a rapt expression.

Lee paused and took in the foreign but beautiful scene. The lodge behind them, the dogs at their kennels, all the paths carved into the deep snow, trees all around, a large open area with trails several hundred yards away, and mountains climbing toward the sky in the distance. Then there was Maverick, standing tall and confident in the middle of it all. The way he fit perfectly in this environment took Lee's breath away.

She was far away from her life in Georgia in more ways than distance.

His gaze was inscrutable behind his sunglasses. He stood mere inches away, puffs of vapor drifting up every few seconds. A chilly breeze whipped around them.

"So, want to take the babies on a walk?"

Chapter Fifteen

M AV GLANCED BACK as Bob pulled Lee along the trail in the vast meadow behind the lodge. Every time they stopped to rest, she'd give unhandsome Bob a scratch behind the ears and tell him how nice he looked.

Mav was not jealous of a dog.

For Lee's ease of trekking, Mav had switched out Bob for Kenai, since Kenai had an ingrained need to lead. Kenai's leash that was attached to Mav's harness was longest and she strode out in front of Klister, Denali, and Kaaktuq, who snacked on snow along the way. The dogs had settled into the activity, no longer barking with excitement, since now they were doing the thing they wanted to do in the first place.

The midday weather had turned, with increased wind signaling the leading edge of tonight's predicted storm. He checked his satellite phone, similar to the one he gave the guests to use for trail emergencies. No messages. The guests might still be in town—they had planned to go out for lunch, supplies, and drinks before returning later this afternoon.

At the far side of the meadow, he stopped his team and waited as Lee caught up to him a minute later. Walking quickly thanks to the one dog-power engine pulling her, Lee had gotten the hang of the hip belt and leash that connected to Bob's harness.

Once she reached him, Mav gave a signal and the dogs all immediately lay down in curled-up balls on the trail. Even retired sled dogs knew to nap at any opportunity.

Man, Lee was adorable, decked out in snow pants that had some shape thanks to the hip belt, a puffy coat she'd partially unzipped to thermoregulate, a neck gaiter that rested below her chin, and a green and red wool beanie that set off her pink cheeks and made her brown eyes glow when she removed her sunglasses in the lower light. If she hated the Alaskan outback, she hid it well.

Why did he assume she'd hate it?

No way would he answer the question. Lee wasn't Skylar.

More to the point, Lee wouldn't be in Yukon Valley forever, and Mav needed to pound that reality into his thick skull.

"Wow," she said for the thousandth time today. Lee rotated in a slow circle. In between wind-driven snow squalls, the lodge appeared as a small dot on the far side of the meadow. Well-used trails diverged at their current location and went hundreds of miles into the wilderness or over to town five miles away. "This place is amazing."

He propped his sunglasses on his head. "I'm really glad you like it."

"Why wouldn't I?"

He hedged, "Not everyone likes the discomfort of cold weather and dealing with smelly dogs."

She popped her free hand on her hip. "Are we back to the part where you think I can't handle things here?"

"I—" Damn it. "No."

"It's one thing to be from somewhere else and hate everything about the unfamiliar place. It's another thing to have new experiences and decide to be happy wherever you land." A puff of vapor escaped her pink lips. "You might not understand that if you've only lived in one place. Or if you've never given anyone a chance to try and enjoy different things and discover for themselves."

"Whoa. That's a lot to process." He put his hands up. "First of all, I've introduced others to this world, and some people didn't like it. Second, my bad for making that early assumption about your lack of ability to live here in Yukon Valley. You're never going to let me live down those comments."

"Nope." Lee stomped a boot. God, she was cute.

He refocused on averting a conversation disaster. "Third of all"—Mav looked down at his motley group of dogs that had gotten him through adventures, near-death experiences, and more than one heartbreak—"I'm sorry."

Lee opened her mouth on a small sound, then closed it. "Pardon?"

"I don't always react in the best way. That's my personal baggage talking. I'll try not to make assumptions."

Narrowing her eyes, she said, "You're a guy being insightful. Is this a trap?"

"I mean it. I know when I'm out of line. Dee reminds me of it every chance she can." He took off the backpack he carried, pulled out two bottles of water, and handed her one. "As for the rest of it, let's say that I've seen firsthand how someone thinks they want to be here with me and the dogs, but then decides that both the *here* parts and the dog parts suck. I wasn't enough to make up for those things."

"Okay, yes. That's rough." She opened the nozzle on the bottle and took a sip, then tilted her head. "The dogs aren't terrible at all. They're quite bunch of characters, but they're still family and they love you for who you are."

"If only all humans were as accepting." The words came out before he could stop them. "Look, that's my junk to carry around. You don't need to know all the details. It's a relationship that sucked. It's done."

Her brown eyebrows rose, like she'd discovered something.

Another few minutes passed, punctuated by the occasional *whuff* of a dog getting more comfortable. Mav hovered nearby but didn't come any closer.

After a few minutes, Lee capped the bottle and handed it back to him. "You're not the only person with baggage."

He stowed the container in the backpack on the ground. "I figured," he said gently.

"Did you now?" she bristled.

Crap. *Backpedal, man.* "You had brought up an ex earlier."

Her shoulders rose and fell. "Ex-husband. He never cared to understand my job, unless it somehow benefitted him." Putting her mitten back over the liner, she flashed a self-deprecating smile. "My value was in how he could use me as a social prop and how he could advance his career with my family's connections. He liked my pocketbook. Too much."

Whistling low, Mav gave her upper arm a quick squeeze. "What a piece of work. What kind of man thinks that your work isn't significant? Or takes advantage of the money you bring in?"

"Any of our jobs in healthcare are important. And not just healthcare. To undermine what a person does, who they are …" She huffed. "Work's not everything. I get it. We all have lives outside of medicine that are meaningful. But wanting someone to participate in their life outside of work is different than degrading the work they're doing."

"What the—" Mav stopped himself. "Never mind. Not going to say what I'm thinking."

"Hey, I picked him. There's not much you can say that I haven't thought." She held up a hand when he opened his mouth. "How we ended up married is a long story that involved my residency training, plus exhaustion and long hours sprinkled with naivete and combined with his excellent acting ability."

"Huh."

"He liked to play the part of a rising local politician. Enjoyed the finer things in life, without looking at the price tags."

"Guessing you supplied those finer things in life?"

"My paycheck sure did, and I was way too busy and way too trusting to realize what he was doing until he had dug us into a hell of a hole. Debt that we couldn't show anyone because it might tarnish his squeaky clean, successful image."

"He sounds swell."

"What you want to say is that I sure picked a winner, huh?" Her dry laugh chilled the air a few more degrees. "Short answer? After we were married, he was not the same guy. Took me a minute to figure it out." She shrugged. "Anyway, that's my baggage. Not that it's a contest at all," Lee said, kicking her boot toe into the hip-deep snow on the side of the trail.

"Not a lot of respect for you or what you did."

She gave another curt nod. "Case in point. Healthcare worker schedule logistics. You and I know that changing schedules are part of the territory and we work around it, and we understand if there are last-minute situations, right? Not my ex. Medical emergencies that cut into his plans or if I was committed to take call on a day he wanted to add a social function, he'd flip out."

Mav rolled a thick gloved hand into a fist. "Not physically."

"No. More like emotional manipulation and meanness." One corner of her mouth dropped. "Well, then there was the cheating. And I mentioned draining my savings account."

"You're kidding."

She shook her head, head ducked but cheeks pink, like she was both embarrassed and pissed. "After the divorce papers were served, he was so mad that he filed a HIPAA whistleblower suit on me, alleging that I had discovered his affair by accessing a patient's chart and reading the chart notes."

His jaw dropped. "What?"

"Apparently, his girlfriend was at some point a patient in my hospital. I had no idea."

"I assume everything got cleared up."

"Totally. With electronic medical records nowadays, every log-in and every click is tracked. I never was in that chart." She rubbed her nose with the back of her mitten.

"This is unreal. I can't believe someone would go to those lengths to hurt you."

At her sad smile, he stepped forward then stopped himself as she drawled, "If I'm lyin', I'm dyin'."

"What does that mean?"

"Means yes, he did those things. And yes, they happened without me knowing at first. Yes, I was a little clueless and too busy to see what was going on." With a jut of her jaw, she added, "But he can't do those things to me anymore."

Mav took a few seconds to pull his thoughts together. Her ex was as useless as moose droppings. It took a real tool to go that deep into the well of asshole-ness.

Of course she felt gun-shy. Exposed. Probably financially vulnerable.

Mav rocked back on his heels as an intense need hit him. He wanted to be the man who proved to Lee that not all men were like that guy. He wanted to be the exact opposite. He wanted to provide for her, even if that only went as far as supporting the work she did.

Also, he wanted five minutes of polite, civil, one-on-one … conversation … with the ex.

Her voice cut through his dark thoughts. "Uh, sorry. I don't normally go into my history. I don't normally vent. It's not fair for you, and it puts a damper on the nice day."

"It's your story to tell. You decide what to tell me. Besides, the day is nice with you in it." He unclenched his rolled fist. "It means a lot that you shared that with me." He rested his gloved hand on her shoulder, needing to anchor his churning thoughts and ground his anger. Needing to support her.

"Um, you, too, for sharing about your past." She gave an icy laugh. "Guess we both have issues we're dealing with." Lee rested her cheek against his hand. He couldn't feel her skin, but the gesture cracked open something inside of his chest.

He squared up to stand close, facing her. "You know that what you do is important, right? You, being here, in Yukon Valley, caring for those patients. It's needed. It's appreciated. No one around here cares if anyone is rich or not. People here just want to make their way in the world, provide for their families, and be successful in whatever they do."

"Um." She dropped eye contact with a suspicious sheen in her gaze.

Tilting her chin up, he added, "I'm glad you're out here with me today."

It killed him when she blinked several times.

She bit her lower lip, then set her jaw in a determined jut. "It's easy to hang out here. This area is peaceful. Your lodge is amazing, and your dogs are fun. Anyone would be happy to be here." She paused. "With you. You're a good guy. You know that, right?"

She was a champ at changing the subject back to him.

But her words, the way she saw him, struck a nerve.

Lee had a tender heart, and Mav knew she was being kind. He recognized that all he had to offer was his rural paramedic work, a failing business, limited cell phone and Wi-Fi access, and a mangy bunch of old sled dogs.

Even so, he still wanted to prove to Lee that she mattered, that there were guys out there who weren't like her ex. Guys like Mav who might not be fancy but for sure appreciated the hell out of the amazing person that she was.

Damn it. He shouldn't.

The pink in her cheeks glowed in the overcast day.

Unable to stop himself, he drew her toward him and dipped his head to kiss her, inhaling the scents of fresh air, tart salmonberry, and a hint of flowers. She sighed against his lips and opened to him, drawing him in deeper. Those profound and altruistic thoughts fled. Within a minute, his brain stopped functioning, and he couldn't tell where he ended and where she began.

The wind whipped around them, but his senses only registered her scent, her taste, her soft skin under his lips. He wanted to move slowly. Take care with her heart. Remind her of her value. Prove his own worth to her and to himself.

He also wanted to explore more of her right now, frostbite be damned.

He kissed the corner of her mouth and tasted ... salt?

As he pulled away, his gut clenched at the track of tears down one cheek. "Lee. Oh gosh. Hey, if I—"

"No, it's me." Her quiet voice cut through the gale.

He carefully wiped the moisture away with his insulated

thumb. "Is that a variation on the it's-me-not-you line?"

She nestled her cheek against his palm for a minute, then peeked up at him. "Sorry. Not sure where all those feelings came from."

"You never need to apologize, Lee. It's okay to feel things out here." Her frame trembled underneath his hands. "Except for cold. Seems like I need to get you out of the weather."

"Your way of warming me up wasn't all bad." The pink on her cheeks deepened and her eyes danced.

His tongue stuck to the roof of his mouth. *Say something. Anything.*

She dropped her gaze and cleared her throat. Moment gone.

At Mav's feet, Kaaktuq shifted, then let out a satisfied *whuff* and a doggy fart.

Moment killed.

Mav and Lee laughed, but a few seconds later, they both recoiled in horror.

"Buddy, seriously, what is wrong with you?" Mav held his hand over his nose.

The dog raised his head and opened his mouth in an unrepentant and largely empty smile.

Lee backpedaled. Bob jumped up, ready to run again, tangling around her legs in his excitement. She tripped on him.

Mav grabbed her by the waist right before she face-planted. When he hauled her upright, her laughter rang out across the meadow, triggering his own grin.

"Are you okay?" he asked.

She waved her hand in front of her face and scrunched up her nose, pointing to Kaaktuq. "It's like a thousand dead fish rotting in the sun. How can something so small and cute create that much stink?"

"Told you he's deadly." He groaned, unable to escape the flatulent dog now tethered to him. "Probably a good time to head back to the lodge."

Chapter Sixteen

AFTER TUCKING IN the babies, Lee, Maverick, and Kenai rounded the corner of the house. The large maroon SUV pulled up in front of the cabin and six men exited, four of them retrieving grocery bags and twelve-packs of beer from the trunk. Hard to tell ages, but it seemed like a few younger twenties guys and the rest older. One of the men in a blue coat that strained over his gut raised his hand in greeting and tromped over in what looked like stiff new boots.

Lee caught Maverick's faint grunt.

The gray light had made things bright enough to require the sunglasses she wore. On instinct, she tugged her neck gaiter up over her nose and made sure her hair was tucked under her beanie.

Mav switched Kenai's lead to his left hand and extended his right for a brief handshake. "Trip to town went okay?" His words came out friendly but tight.

The man, maybe in his late forties, grinned and patted his belly. "Tried out the local diner and then got some provisions for this weekend. Damn, but prices are expensive here! Nothing like Boise. Even when I met the boys to drive up from Anchorage the other day, it was cheaper there."

Lee studied the man in his very puffy jacket. Wonder why he didn't fly into Fairbanks? Who chose to drive all the way from Anchorage to Yukon Valley in winter?

Not her business. Lee shivered. She just wanted to warm up.

Maverick nodded. "It's true. All the groceries have to be shipped in from longer distances. In rural Alaska, we pay more for sundries and food. We pay nothing in income tax, so that helps."

"Ha." The man peered around. "Not much benefit if there's no income."

Lee's head whipped up. What the heck?

Next to her Maverick stiffened. She bristled along with him.

"Pardon," Maverick finally gritted out.

The guy's smile. Somehow it was wrong. "I meant that you don't likely get much business way out here."

"I get enough." Mav's tone dropped another few notes. "Well. I don't want to keep you."

Wind gusted snow around them, and Lee stomped a cold foot. Temperature was dropping, not all due to the conversation in front of her. She scanned the low clouds and snow scudding across the plowed parking area.

The grocery-carrying guys had disappeared into their cabin. The remaining man, tall but younger, wearing a heavy winter coat, headed for the entrance of the lodge.

"I'll be ready in ten, Randy," he called out, opening the front door.

"Roger." Randy turned back to Maverick. "We're going

to get a ride in before the snow. Hope those older snowmobiles are safe and up to the task."

Waves of tension poured off of Maverick. Kenai's tail didn't move. What was going on here?

The wind whipped at Maverick's words. "I personally tuned up all the snow*machines* this past week. Even the extra one." She caught the difference in terminology. Must be an Alaska thing.

Randy turned in a one-hundred-eighty-degree arc around him. His expression was assessing but not appreciative. "Yeah, Nick decided to tag along at the last minute. Lucky you had the extra guest rooms available for him and for me. With everyone else in the cabin, it's nice to spread out." He eyed Lee. "Who is this lady with you?"

Suppressing a cringe, she said, "Hello, I'm Lee." Her voice muffled behind the gaiter.

"You live here?" Randy's sparse eyebrows rose. Above his ruddy cheeks, weathered lines formed. He should have appeared jolly, but the impression she got from him was *trying too hard.* Calculating. He had a hard edge, and she couldn't figure him out.

"Nope," she said, equally as brief as Maverick. She didn't want to give more details than absolutely necessary.

Maverick gave an empty, polite laugh. "Lee and I work together."

"What do you do?" the man asked.

As Lee opened her mouth, Maverick interrupted, "I'm a paramedic in town."

"Oh. Hmm." He nodded, focusing immediately on

Maverick.

"Well," he said, jiggling Kenai's leash. "Be careful out there. Weather's coming in, blowing hard from the west. Take your GPS. Visibility can change quickly. Come to think of it, you may not want to go out today."

"As long as the snowmobiles don't break, we'll be fine." He preceded them to the front door and walked in, not stopping to take off his boots. "Besides, I don't want to waste the free fuel in the machines. Catch you later, boss." Dots of snow dropped from his boot lugs and speckled the rugs and floor as he walked to the guest wing. A door slammed.

A muscle in Maverick's jaw popped. In various situations over the past three weeks, she had never observed him angry. Even in the Code Blue, he stayed calm and loose. This man in front of her stood stiffly, as if a steel pipe ran though his spine.

Lee sat and unlaced her boots, patting Kenai on the head until she got a tail wag. "That was strange." She pitched her voice low.

He bent and took off his boots, tucking them on the rubber mat beneath the entry bench. Removing his woolen beanie, he finger-combed his hair and glared at the guest rooms.

"Something about those guys hits me the wrong way. I can't put my finger on it." He hung his coat on the peg and fished out the satellite phone from a pocket.

Lee stood and hung her coat up then patted his arm. "I agree. I get weird vibes. Nothing scary, but kind of … off."

His lips thinned, and he snaked an arm around her,

tucking her into his side for a beat. "Dad always told me to trust my gut."

"Forget the gut. I'd trust your mutt." She pointed to Kenai, whose muted demeanor spoke volumes.

"True. She's a good judge of character." He patted Kenai on the head, and she trotted over to her nap location in front of the embers still warming the fireplace grate. Drawing Lee with him, he peered from the great room in the direction of the guest wing. "Sorry that none of this is what we'd planned. Activities not as advertised," he intoned.

An impulse prompted her to keep her snow pants on as well as the vest over her long-sleeve Capilene thermal top.

"I enjoyed everything about today's adventure so far. It's been fun hanging out together." She kept her beanie on, too, then sat cross-legged and sideways on one of the couches, propping her back against the armrest and facing the fireplace.

Maverick remained standing next to her, posture tense. Vigilant.

A snowmobile—no, snowmachine—rumbled, joined by another. Soon, four engines ran outside the door. Randy and Nick tromped back through the great room with *thuds* of boots and harsh rasps of waterproof outdoor clothing material.

"Later, folks," Randy said, barely sparing them a glance as he barreled out of the house.

"You have your SAT phone just in case?" Maverick asked, holding his up.

He patted his pocket. "Right here, boss."

The door slammed as they exited. Soon, more engines added to the din. Then the noise changed from a fading rumble into a higher-pitched buzz as they exited the property and increased their speeds into the distance.

Maverick stared out the great room windows with a dark scowl. At the point where she was about to get up and give him a hug, he turned. "I should offer you a drink or snacks."

With a snort, she said, "You seem like the one who needs a drink."

"No kidding. But not while I'm on the clock."

"Water is fine for me." She set the beanie on the coffee table and ran her hands through her tangled hair.

"Water. Got it." He groaned. "Man, I'm not the best host today." He went to the kitchen and brought back full glasses and placed each one on a coaster on top of the end tables. "Let me know if you want anything else." With a tired grunt, he dropped heavily onto the couch next to her.

She studied his tense profile. "So, why is this group so important? And what was all that earlier rooster strutting from that Randy guy?"

Not answering right away, he leaned over and picked up her legs, setting them down on his lap. His palms rested on her knees, the comfortable weight warming her even through the winter clothing layers. "Not sure about Randy's deal." He patted her leg. "I'm not a big fan of airing personal laundry."

"Did you not see me do that exact thing an hour ago? My laundry, *bleeeah*, there it went. Right at your feet. Totally aired out."

He did a quarter turn toward her, his thigh muscles bunching beneath her legs as he shifted. "Lee, I'm happy to listen to anything you want to tell me, anytime."

"Same."

Running a hand over his hair, he nodded. "Dee and I inherited this property, the lodge, the cabins, the snow-machines, all of it, about four years ago. After Mom and Dad died. Once she and I finished estate matters and processed our grief, we decided to keep it in the family and carry on our parents' dream to turn the place into a guest lodge."

"Which you've done," she said, holding her two palms up.

He draped the arm closest to her over the back of the couch, blunt fingertips tapping the supple leather upholstery. "It's been challenging working as EMS director and getting the business off the ground. There's always something that needs to be fixed, and even though we've made booking cabins or a room easy with the online portal through the website, availability is limited due to my EMS schedule."

"What about Dee?"

"She helps where she can, but with her role at the hospital, most of her time is spent there. Also, she's still working through her other grief, which was the loss of her husband five years ago."

"Oh boy. It's been tough for both of you."

"We have each other, which helps." He absently rubbed her leg. "We've gotten behind on the mortgage. My folks purchased this main lodge about ten years ago, with the smaller cabins and the guest wing added shortly before they died. The mortgage for this much land, a large house, added to the construction loans for those three cabins? Even in the middle of nowhere in Alaska, it's considerable. Mom and Dad had been pouring every spare dime into the place." His facial features appeared carved from stone.

"Guessing that you and Dee contribute what you can."

"Yes, but it's not enough. I mean, we do okay, but she needs to save for her retirement. Me, too, I guess. We have good rural jobs, but they don't pay like city jobs." With defensive heat, he said, "Yes, that's a choice we made, staying out here." He heaved a lungful of air in and slowly exhaled. "Sorry. I know that you understand."

Lee knew all about having nothing in savings, a nonexistent retirement account, and a staggering amount of loans. She also had a good understanding of the economic realities of living in a rural area. Although in her situation, the hospital paid a premium to bring her in to urgently cover the full scope of services here. Still. She laced fingers with his on the back of the couch. "Sometimes it's good to talk about it."

He gave her a tight smile. "So, to answer your original question, every guest visit is important, not only for the lodge's online reviews and publicity but also for the income."

"Makes sense."

"What's adding pressure, besides the looming bank default"—his Adam's apple bobbed—"there have been offers from a potential buyer lately."

She squeezed his hand. "Guessing you've told them no."

"It's a big decision either way, and Dee's wavering. I'm not ready to let it go. But if we go into foreclosure, then the bank can make the decision to sell it to them. Right out from under us."

"That's a terrible feeling."

"You have no idea."

Actually, Lee had a pretty good idea. At least she no longer had to cover the monthly lake cabin payments. *How's that working out for you, Preston? Creditors calling yet?*

She mentally shook her head and focused on what Maverick was saying.

"Even though these guests are rough around the edges, I need for them to have a great time, tell their friends, put it on social media, and come back soon. That's my whole business plan in a nutshell, with the dream that we might get someone famous to stay here and a review goes viral one day. When we don't have a ton of customers, each encounter is that much more important. It's stressful." Maverick's blue gaze locked on to her, stealing her breath for a split second. "Now I'd like to forget about that junk and move on to other topics."

Lee leaned forward and pulled his hand resting on the back of the couch toward her, rubbing her cheek against his rough palm. For some reason, she needed to maintain physical contact with him in this quiet space. How much of that desire was due to feeling raw after she revealed her history with Preston and hinted at her financial issues out in the meadow? Or due to wanting to support Maverick? Or was it because of a need to explore the growing connection between them?

She dropped her hand, allowing him the choice to move

his away.

He cupped her jaw in the palm of his hand.

Her heart stumbled.

"If you need time and space, I understand. I can leave you to your work." She said the words because she felt they were necessary to say, not because she wanted to say them.

Maverick scooted closer and slid his hand over her cheek, sinking his fingers into her hair and sending tingles over her scalp. "You leaving is precisely what I *don't* need." He went still. "Unless it's you who would like to go, and I wouldn't blame you." His chuckle came from a few inches away. "Look at our rock-solid confidence, giving each other mutual outs."

Smiling, she said, "What if we're not confident enough to take those outs?"

"I'm happy right here with you. *Confident* that I'm happy." He massaged her scalp with his warm fingers, and she sighed, leaning into his touch.

"I'll be very happy, too, especially if you keep that up."

The first full laugh she'd heard in a while came from deep in his chest. "I'll get a good Yelp review, then?" he said.

"At least four and a half stars."

His brows shot up. "What if I want to get five stars?"

Lee froze, thoughts tumbling through her logical brain. God, she wanted to explore more of ... whatever this was with Maverick. The banter, the gentle and sexy teasing, the possibility of more. She stared at him. "I—"

His voice slid over her like a soft, warm blanket. "What do you want, Lee? Don't overthink it. This isn't life or death."

"But." Her mind whirled with things past and present and future. "You. Me?"

"Let me start. I want to kiss you more if you're okay with it."

Don't overthink it. Lee knelt on the couch, steadying herself on his shoulders and locking eyes with him as he gripped under her butt to boost her onto his lap. "Maybe we can get that extra half star if we continue what we were doing when Kaaktuq tried to fumigate us?" she asked.

He removed the satellite phone from a leg pocket and set it on the arm of the couch. Then he positioned her knees on either side of his thighs and then he lifted his hands. "Be my guest. Literally."

Her laugh turned into a low hum as their lips met in an air-stealing kiss. Lee wrapped one arm around his neck and fisted her other hand into his shirt, hanging on while he changed angles.

She could have let go completely and the iron bands of his arms snaking around her back and waist would have held her securely against his chest. His fingers pressing into her flesh triggered pressure deep in her pelvis, and she let herself sink deeper onto his hard thighs.

Toying with the strands at his nape, she enjoyed the silky slide of his hair through her fingers. Under her roving hand, the muscles of his neck grew taut, as if formed from metal. An Alaskan mountain man, indeed. All fresh air, ruggedness, and steely strength.

But gentle. He held back the strength. Let her set the

pace.

This man could not be any more different than any man she'd known before.

Lee stifled any inner debate. What did she want? The answer was simple. She enjoyed spending time with Maverick. She wanted to experience more of his strength, more of him, up close and personal.

By the growling rumbles coming from his throat and how he clenched his hands on her hips, he shared her interest.

Are we good? the vulnerable part of herself she protected the most asked.

Oh yes. We are good.

The sweep of his tongue over hers tilted the world around her, until she realized that he had eased her back onto the couch and bracketed her head with his hands. Maverick pressed his torso against hers but kept his full weight off of her with a foot planted on the floor.

Lee lifted her hips off the couch, craving the pressure of his body. She shifted restlessly, tugging him down to her, gripping his corded upper arms. She was so warm beneath him, in her outdoor gear.

He continued the sensual onslaught of kisses, dragging his lips over hers, then licking his way down her neck and back up again. His warm spruce and fresh air scent was laced with the hint of aftershave, and she inhaled deeply.

At one point, he nudged her head to one side and nipped at an earlobe—not enough to hurt, but enough to make her squeal. Hearing his rapid breaths and growls so close sent delicious quivers straight into her belly. Everything about him was so intimate, so immediate.

For a moment, Lee froze as a wave of vulnerability shook her limbs. There it was again. Self-doubt paralyzing her.

Did she trust herself to make a good decision?

Lee had to be okay with the current situation, regardless of any long-term plans for either of them. Regardless of her history.

Regardless of her fear.

She breathed deep once, twice. His scent both focused and excited her. This felt right. Safe.

Sexy.

God, Lee wanted to feel good in his arms. Wanted to trust that he would care about her. Care *for* her.

She wanted to trust that she would choose someone who wouldn't hurt her. That realization jolted her back to reality.

She couldn't move.

After a few more seconds, the kisses stopped. He pulled his head back. "Lee? Hey, are you all right?" His voice was rough, and he exhaled like he'd run a race. "Talk to me."

"This feels so good. It's a lot to process. Are you okay? I mean, with this," she whispered. "It's not too much? Too fast?" Without thinking about the motion, she scraped her nails over his scalp.

He lowered his hips and rocked against hers, groaning along with her. The friction and pressure weren't enough. Not by a long shot.

The cords in his neck flexed and relaxed. "I can't explain it." His respiratory rate slowed as he dropped his forehead to hers. "Never been one to jump into things." He barked a laugh. "With you? I'll ski off the edge of an unknown cliff right this minute." He locked his elbows, holding himself away, watching her. "That's not to say we have to take this any further. No pressure."

"It's both of our decisions."

His jaw clenched and he growled his response. "I already know my answer."

In this cocoon surrounded by cushions and his arms, Lee studied the fine weathered lines of his face and the slash of his firm and sensual mouth wet with their kisses.

She bit her lip. "Would you?"

"Would I what?"

"Want to go further than just kisses?" she whispered.

"Hell. Yes." He bit off the words like a piece of jerky. "How about you? We're both grown adults. We can decide together to stop or go. Both choices are right."

"Are we voting?"

"Sure, but if there's a tie, you get the tiebreaker, Lee."

A heady swirl of self-determination, confidence, and anticipation coiled in her belly. "I vote … yes! Onward and upward."

He threw his head back and laughed, then dropped back down for another kiss that went on and on until her head spun. His hand drifted down to her waist, and he worked his fingers under the layers of her clothes until the rough pads of his fingers grazed her skin. Goosebumps rose beneath his touch.

Slipping his hand back out, he huffed a half curse,

grabbed the hem of her Capilene top and vest, and scooted the garments up.

Sitting back on his knees, he pressed his hands to her abdomen and slid them over her simple bra, cupping the undersides of her breasts.

"Damn it," he muttered, pushing the material higher and failing.

"What?"

His feral scowl made her shiver. "You have way too many layers on."

With a shaky laugh, she winked. "Sounds like an Alaska problem."

"It's one I intend to solve." He slipped his hands out from under her garments and unzipped her vest, pushing the thicker fabric to the sides. Then he lifted the thin Capilene shirt hem up to her upper chest, sliding the bra off with it. The first touch of his hands on her breasts set off a spark of desire, hotter than a roaring fire in the hearth. He palmed the fullness of each breast, then squeezed until she gave a desperate squeak.

With rough thumbs and index fingers, he pinched her nipples, rolling them. Liquid heat pooled at the junction of her thighs. She gripped his upper arms. If he weren't anchoring her to the couch, she might have gone into orbit with the sensual touch.

"Oh my God." She gasped.

A chirping sound reached her from the periphery of coherent thought.

He bent his head to suck one tight nub into his mouth,

flicking his tongue over the tip. Squirming, she arched her back.

The high-pitched sound continued, and she struggled to identify it.

"Maverick," she panted. He moved to her other breast and sensations bloomed brighter and hotter. "Oh, my—"

More chirping. An electronic sound.

"Maverick."

"What, Lee? Are you okay?" He stopped, eyelids at half mast, lips damp, hands clamped on her breasts. He blinked and looked at the coffee table. "Damn. It." Launching himself off of her, he grabbed the satellite phone on the end table. "Yeah," his voice came out harshly.

Moments passed. Words she couldn't make out came through the phone.

Her skin cooled where he had licked her. Lee reset her bra, pulled her top and vest down, and sat on the couch, taking deep gulps of air. She detected Maverick's scent every time she inhaled. Touching her tingling lips, she watched as he paced.

"Where are you?" A pause. "What's his condition?"

Oh no.

"Don't move him," he said, in take-charge paramedic mode. "Call 911 to mobilize local EMS backup. Tell dispatch I'll be at the site soon." He ended the call.

"What's going on?"

His thunderous expression made her lean from him. "One of the guests crashed on the trail."

Chapter Seventeen

DAMN IT ALL to hell.

Mav shook loose the cobwebs of passion from his brain as he quickly changed gears to devise a rescue plan. One look at Lee's swollen lips and wide eyes sent another wave of lust that turned his knees to jelly.

He had a job to do. Respond to the injured person on the trail. No time to deal with feelings for the woman sitting two feet away from him. No time to consider that depending on the outcome of the accident he might be looking at the end of his business. No time for anything other than the task in front of him.

Lee stood, hands out. "I can help. What do you need?"

You.

He scrubbed his face.

He couldn't think of any way a date could turn out worse than today. "You don't have to do this. Head on home."

"I'm helping." She popped her hands on her hips. "Hippocratic oath and all."

In spite of the situation, Mav smiled. He loved that she was willing to jump in, no matter the situation. "Put on all of your gear." They walked to the entryway.

In silence punctuated by grunts while they bent down to shimmy into winter clothing and shove feet into boots, they were ready in minutes. His mind spun out logistics and various scenarios at lightning speed as he muttered curses.

Location. About four miles out. The guests had been heading back to the lodge when the accident occurred.

Local EMS or search and rescue assist. Not likely or timely due to location.

Access. He scanned the parking area. Even though the machines could carry two people apiece, the six guests had taken all six machines.

Transport. He prayed his team would be ready to pull for him. "Kenai, here, girl." She trotted over, tail wagging, and stood still as he put on her pink harness.

As they exited the house, he grabbed the other harnesses and bag of booties hanging in the entryway. He checked his watch. 2:35 p.m. Another few hours of light. He stepped back in and retrieved two headlamps hanging on pegs, handing one to Lee.

The wind hit him full blast, driving thin gusts of snow in icy stings on his exposed skin. Lee yanked the neck gaiter up over her nose, pulled the coat's hood over her beanie, shoved on her sunglasses, and zipped everything up. No exposed skin. Good.

He raced to his truck to retrieve the spare EMS kit he kept there, then caught up to Lee and Kenai at the kennel area. The dogs yapped and howled, picking up on the energy.

"Can you put their booties on?" he shouted over the

wind. If the wind kept up, the weather could change into a blizzard and the potential for zero visibility. A deadly situation. He had to trust his dogs to get them out and back in one piece.

"Got it." She knelt and started working on the nearest dog.

Mav dropped the bag and harnesses and hurried to the shed. Inside, the howl of the wind dropped. His ears rang. On the wall nearby he took down an old wooden backboard with worn straps he'd used in the past when he taught wilderness first aid courses. That would do.

The shed held three different winter sleds and a summer cart. He selected the fiberglass expedition sled with the longer cargo bed. He snagged the mushing gear bag hanging on the wall. After dragging the sled over to Lee and the dogs, he set the snow claw to anchor the sled in place, then quickly attached the dogs' harnesses and tuglines to the main gangline secured on the front of the sled. He patted the pocket that held the satellite phone and checked his watch again: 2:46.

Time to go. He placed the backboard in the cargo bed.

"Hop in." He pointed for Lee to climb on top of the flat backboard. When he dropped the EMS bag in front of her, she drew her knees up to fit. "Ready?" he hollered.

"Yes." The word whipped away in the wind, but he saw her mittened thumbs-up.

Stepping on the runners and gripping the handle bow, he pulled the claw and called out, "Kenai. Ready. Hike!" They lurched forward as all five dogs eagerly lunged into their harnesses, and the sled began sliding over the snowy path.

Lee grabbed the top rail of the cargo bed. This trip was not how he wanted to introduce her to the joy of dogsledding. Normally, he tempered the dogs' speed, but not today. A short trip to the scene of an emergency meant that after a five-minute moderate warm-up trot, he would let his dogs run at a quicker pace. Through the whipping wind, he peered down at Lee. She had buried her head in the circle of her arms propped on her bent knees. They raced across the meadow and beyond.

Within twenty minutes, snowmachines and men standing nearby appeared from the swirl of blowing snow and low white daylight that made everything flat and colorless.

"Whoa!" he yelled, and Kenai slowed down to a walk.

The team followed suit, then stopped at his command, yapping and puffing in the cold air before lying down in furry napping lumps.

After dropping the snow claw, Mav hefted the EMS bag onto his shoulder and hurried over to assess the situation. Lee, the front of her hat, coat hood, and neck gaiter all rimed with snow, clambered out of the cargo bed right behind him, hauling the backboard with her.

Five upright snowmachines were parked in a line on the side of the trail. The sixth snowmachine rested upside down with Nick lying on the ground nearby. His helmet had been removed. At a quick glance, Mav didn't notice scratches or dents on the headgear.

"How are you, Nick?" Mav began his assessment.

Nick heaved in big breaths, moaning when he moved.

"Not great. It's my leg."

Airway and breathing? Yes. Mav yanked off his glove and checked Nick's carotid pulse. Regular and strong.

His primary assessment did not show any overt deformities, but unstable joints and occult injuries weren't always obvious. Also, one injury could distract from other serious problems. In the cold temperatures, he couldn't fully expose Nick for a more thorough evaluation. He had Nick wiggle his feet and hands and answer a few questions. Pupils were equal and reactive. Neurologic status grossly intact without deficits. That was good news.

Kneeling, he pressed his bare hands against Nick's body from head to toe, reaching under his back to palpate the back and spine. When he got to the right leg, Nick yelled.

"Can you get the SAM splint?" he asked Lee.

She knelt and unzipped the EMS bag, digging until she found the moldable splint.

"Did anyone see anything? How fast were you all going?" he asked.

"No idea. The snowmobile must have malfunctioned. You're liable for this, you know," Randy sneered. The other men shrugged and shook their heads.

Mav gritted his teeth. "I need to know mechanism of injury. Speed. Direction. Obstacles. Did you hit something, Nick? How did you land on the ground?"

Nick squinted up at Randy then back to Mav. "Not sure. Wasn't supposed to happen like this—"

"What he means," Randy interrupted, "is that the throttle got stuck and the machine threw him off right before hitting the tree." He spat into the snow. "Shoddy vehicle maintenance. Unsafe trail conditions. You should have never let us go out this afternoon."

What the hell?

At that moment, Mav envisioned his entire business going up in proverbial smoke. Didn't matter that the men had signed numerous waivers of liability, promising to take responsibility for damage to the vehicles and any personal injuries. Didn't matter that Mav had warned them about the weather issues this afternoon. The customer's perception became their reality, and Randy had decided that this whole thing was somehow Mav's fault.

His business's reputation would be ruined. No income meant no mortgage payments.

No mortgage payments meant that he was going to lose his family property. Right here with this accident.

Mav pushed back a queasy churning in his gut. Later. He'd deal with the fallout later. Right now, he had to help Nick.

He turned to Lee. "Mechanism of injury, moderate-speed crash without loss of consciousness. Spine precautions before immobilizing his leg."

She nodded with an unreadable expression due to her hood, sunglasses, and gaiter protecting her face against the wind-driven snow. She positioned the board next to Nick and scooted behind him to provide in-line neck support. As Mav secured the leg splint, Lee murmured questions to Nick as a way to continue monitoring his breathing and cognitive status.

"Let's logroll," he said to Lee.

"Okay," she said in her muffled voice. She leaned forward. "Hang on. We might be able to clear his spine clinically."

"Good idea." He ran through the algorithm. Mechanism of injury was significant impact, which was a higher risk for spine injury. No loss of consciousness. He did have a distracting injury in the leg, which complicated the assessment.

"Have you been drinking?"

"No," Nick said. "We were going to have some drinks afterward."

"Any drug use?" he asked.

"Hey!" Randy snapped. "Why are you asking him those questions? It's none of your business."

Mav shouted back, "These questions are part of the paramedic injury assessment for complicating factors. If you're not going to help me, then stand back."

Lee's head whipped up. He could imagine her eyes going wide. Mav rarely yelled at anyone.

She murmured something to Nick and slid her hand under each side of his neck.

"No pain," he said.

"Can you move it on your own?" she asked.

He gingerly flexed, extended, and rotated his head without difficulty or pain.

"That's good." She patted him on the shoulder and sent Mav another thumbs-up. "C-spine cleared per criteria."

Liability being what it was, he knew the ER doc would

still scan everything from head to pelvis, out of an abundance of caution. Of course, they would keep movement to a minimum en route to the hospital.

Mav projected volume behind his words. "I need one of you to help us with this backboard." Another guest moved forward as Randy took a step back. "When I tell you, slide the board underneath him and keep all of the straps free. One, two, three."

As one, he and Lee rolled Nick. The guest pushed the board under, then they eased Nick onto the board. Lee pulled out a reflective emergency blanket and tucked it over Nick's coat, then they quickly secured the straps.

With the other riders helping, they lifted Nick strapped to the backboard and set him in the sled's cargo bed.

As Mav prepared to leave, he asked the guests, "Can one of you follow us and give her a ride to the hospital?"

Randy puffed out his chest. "Sure, I'll do it." He bent and handed her Nick's discarded helmet.

Mav really didn't like that her safety depended on a guy who wanted to sue him.

No other choice.

"Don't follow too closely or you'll spook the dogs," he told Randy. "Guys, can the rest of you make your way back to the cabin? Or do you want to follow us to town?" They called out confidence in reaching the lodge, and he ensured they had trail maps and GPS coordinates set. The wind had died down over the past ten minutes, visibility improved.

He looked at his watch. 3:41. Not a bad rate of extraction, considering. From this location, they were about seven miles away from town. About a half hour run for the dogs.

Before leaving, he motioned Lee over and gave her the satellite phone. "Can you call the ahead for the trauma alert? A 911 operator may have done it when we first called, but they won't know the latest details or timing to tell the hospital."

"Sure thing." She patted his upper arm and said with that muffled voice, "Good job dealing with this mess, by the way." Walking away from the men, she held the phone to her ear.

Her voice faded to nothing as he drove his sled away.

Chapter Eighteen

ABOUT FORTY MINUTES later, Lee dismounted at the ED entrance and handed the helmet back to Randy. Staff was already transferring Nick from the sled to a gurney.

Maverick's shoulders drooped as he glanced her way. The sun had set and twilight cast his face in shadows. "I'm headed over to the ambulance garage to water the dogs."

"I'll see if folks need help in the ED," she said, handing him the satellite phone.

"Should I wait for you?" His voice was as flat as the low ambient light around them.

"No. Take care of the babies. I'll get a ride back later."

"Sure." He shook his head. "We were done anyway." He grasped Kenai's neckline and slowly trudged across the parking lot with the team and the attached sled.

Her chest ached at the sight of this rugged man, believing that his dreams had been broken in a matter of moments. For a person who fixed problems for a living, she didn't have an answer to this situation.

As staff wheeled Nick into the building, Lee followed, turning sideways to sneak in the sliding doors. No staff badge on her today.

The doors closed on Randy's big, gaping mouth. He

could stay outside for all she cared. Or he could sit in the waiting area and think about new ways to be a jerk.

She gritted her teeth.

Lee needed to change clothes and assist in the ED. When she had spoken with Amberlyn before leaving the accident site, it sounded like the on-call doc, Paul, was busy with a difficult labor and likely couldn't break away.

Snagging a generic staff badge from the HUC, she headed into the locker room, shucked off the winter gear, and pulled on fresh scrubs. Thank goodness she kept an extra pair of labor shoes in her locker. The fit of her thick wool-socked feet into the well-worn Danskos was tight, but it worked. Without a hat on, her hair stood up in strange angles, and so she snagged a patterned cloth bouffant cap and shoved all of her hair beneath it.

Shrugging into her lab coat and looping her stethoscope over her neck, she entered the first trauma bay. Lee reviewed the nursing initial assessment. Vitals were all stable. Neuro status reassuring. That was a great start.

"Let's not move him too much until imaging is done." She and the nurses unstrapped Nick and eased his arms out of the coat and fleece and unzipped the sides of his snow pants, stopping to remove the SAM splint on the lower leg before replacing it over his base thermal underwear layer. Then they carefully rolled him, allowing Lee to do a proper spine palpation. The nurses eased the garments out from under him with an impressive lack of jostling.

However, that small movement must have hurt. "I need something for my pain!" Nick hollered. "Please! This leg is killing me."

Fair enough. A broken leg was miserable. "Amberlyn, please place an IV. Let's give five milligrams of morphine IV. Can you pull rainbow labs?" Rainbow labs meant filling one of every color blood tube to have on hand until Lee knew which orders she wanted. For certain, she would run a tox screen and blood-alcohol level, which could contain key information if litigation occurred. If the lab was drawn after administering morphine, it could result in a false positive flag for opiates. Lee wanted accurate information today. Everything by the books. Nick's health depended on it.

Maverick's future depended on it.

"Got the blood." Amberlyn handed the tubes to the waiting lab tech who stuck labels on and left. Then Amberlyn pushed the morphine dose through the IV hub.

Lee said, "I'd like a CT, head to butt, for a stat teleradiology read. And an x-ray of that leg." With Nick's coat and fleece jacket and snow pants removed, it was easier for her to do a more in-depth exam.

She listened again with her stethoscope. Good air movement in the lungs and a regular heart rate without any rubs to indicate traumatic pericardial effusion. She also pressed on his shoulders, arms, abdomen, and pelvis. No pain.

Then Nick's breathing sped up.

He waved his hand. "Hey, wait. Did you say CT? Is that the donut thing?" His pitch rose. "I'm claustrophobic. I can't go in there! I can't breathe in it!" He clawed at his neck and waved off nursing attempts to hold still as he thrashed. "Where's Randy? This wasn't part of the deal."

Oh boy.

Lee had a choice. Get inadequate imaging and be unable to rule out major internal, spine, or head injuries. Or give a strong antianxiety medication, recognizing that if he had a head injury, it would be difficult to obtain accurate neurologic status assessments.

The twenty-something-year-old patient wailed and thrashed, sitting up on the bed, moving nurses along with him. Looked neurologically intact from here.

Risks versus benefits. "Two milligrams of Versed, please, Amberlyn."

Within a few minutes of receiving the medication, Nick began to relax, and his breathing evened out. Vitals remained stable.

The nurses and radiology tech wheeled Nick back for imaging, while Lee sat in the work area to chart, draping her white coat on the back of the chair.

Where was the on-call doc, Paul? She called out to labor and delivery only to find out that he was considering a vacuum-assisted delivery, with the OR crew en route for possible C-section if the vacuum wasn't successful. Nope, he wasn't coming to the ED anytime soon.

She refreshed the chart on the screen. No uploaded films yet. Lee stared toward the double doors to the waiting area. As much as she disliked Randy, she should give him a quick update. He was probably worried about his nephew.

As she approached the waiting area, she spied him on the phone, pacing. Late afternoon, on this Saturday, only a few visitors drifted in and out through the main entrance doors.

"As long as Nick plays along, we're golden. Uh-huh. This is gonna be money. Literally." He glanced at her and continued to walk and talk. Nothing about his expression suggested that he recognized her.

Because she looked like any generic healthcare worker in the same scrubs and surgical cap as everyone else.

Back at the house and on the trail, he hadn't seen her face.

Mav had implied that she was an EMT. Not a hospital worker.

There was no receptionist on duty this Saturday to identify her. She considered the ring-bell-for-nurse sign next to the ED registration desk, close to where Randy paced.

Lee's heart jumped, but she ducked her head and walked with purpose through the waiting area to the empty nurse triage room and sat at the desk like she worked there.

Activating the intercom button, she listened intently. Randy's voice drifted back to her. "Yeah, with the lawsuit, we're going to get it this time. When I'm done, it'll be pennies on the dollar. From there on out, it'll be pure profit."

A wave of ice worked through her veins. No way. Lee must have misheard. Must be imagining a connection.

They couldn't have faked the injury for litigation. Keeping the intercom open so that she could hear the conversation, she did her best triage nurse impression and acted like this room was her entire job. She logged into the computer on the desk and moved the mouse around. Then she pulled up the x-ray. Yep. Midshaft tibial fracture.

Nothing fake about that finding.

"Oh, he'll be fine." Randy's voice came though the intercom.

He was one of those people who didn't realize how loudly they were talking or didn't care because they thought that it made them sound important. Too bad she would use his loud mouth to her advantage.

"It was more damage than we planned, but that's even better." He paused and sniffed. "Sure, we'll give him a little extra for his trouble. Nick's my nephew. I'll make it his birthday gift."

Lee studied the ceiling at the fisheye that hid the security camera for the small room in which she sat. There was at least one camera in every area of the hospital, recording images and audio 24/7. Even in the waiting room. Could she request footage? Or record Randy?

Doing so might be a crime.

Thanks to her ex's false claim against her to her previous employer, Lee had next-level knowledge regarding patient privacy law. In Georgia, digital images with security cameras could be recorded, but it was a felony to record a private conversation in a private place. There was a recent case involving a hospital where the court interpreted that felony to include recordings of private conversations on medical facility premises.

Problem was, Lee didn't know Alaska's law, and now wasn't the time for legal research.

If she obtained any sort of recording of Randy and it was a crime in this state, she risked being charged with a felony and the evidence thrown out. Also, doctors convicted of a felony couldn't participate in Medicare and state Medicaid programs and couldn't obtain hospital privileges, which would effectively end her ability to work as a physician.

She froze, heart hammering beneath her ribs.

Flashbacks of being called up to the chief medical officer's office back in Georgia, along with the HR director, and the hospital's CEO raced through her mind. She hadn't done anything wrong then, and still Preston had almost gotten her fired because of the HIPAA violation claim.

She walked a tightrope without a net here in Yukon Valley. If she ran afoul of HIPAA law, there would be no do-overs. No more locums assignments. No income.

Over the intercom, Randy kept bragging.

God, she hated bullies.

But she needed her job.

Damn it.

Her palms sweated. So. What *could* she do that was legal?

Lee sat up straighter and looked at the answer right in front of her on the computer screen. The medical record.

She was the treating physician. She could document into the medical record any information *regarding her patient* that pertained to the condition being treated.

Documenting a history of present illness complete with relevant quotes from the patient or others who were present during the injury wasn't a crime. Lee grinned, even as adrenaline zipped heated jolts through her. Careful documentation was not a crime at all—it was part of thorough medical care.

Hate to miss any details that could help my patient, right?

Nearly breathless with her plan, Lee pressed a finger to her lips and listened in as Randy continued his conversation. The topic had changed to travel logistics down to Anchorage. She took in a few slow breaths, waiting for him to cycle back to Nick's part in the scam.

If she recorded damning information in the patient chart, then what?

Nothing that could harm her but also nothing she could share. Legally, she could not pass along her knowledge that the patient was going to sue Maverick. Doing so would violate HIPAA.

Lee knew those HIPAA rules far too well. Only the staff who were officially assigned to care for Nick could discuss details of his case without his explicit permission. No other healthcare worker was allowed to access the chart. Including Maverick, because he was not acting as an official EMS provider.

She drummed her fingers on the laminate tabletop. However.

If Randy's lawsuit went forward, its success would hinge on the medical record. Any mention of an injury depended on the doctor's exam as evidence. Sometimes even a doctor's testimony in court. She knew that fact from working on patients' disability claims over the years.

Her palms sweated.

She had to remain objective. First and foremost, she had to care for her patient and make sound clinical assessments and provide high-quality care. His health came first. She double-checked the CT images. Not ready to view yet.

Time to return to the chart documentation basics. She smiled to herself. Intro to Clinical Practice, first year of medical school, day one—history of present illness.

Lee would take a complete history from her patient. *Very* complete. She would document his responses to her medical questions in the chart. As a physician caring for a trauma victim, she *should* add pertinent clinical information relevant to this patient's case.

Pertinent clinical information, such as direct quotes from other witnesses regarding the accident. Mitigating factors.

Factual statements could help better understand what led up to the accident. The mechanism of injury. The mental state of the patient and those around him. This entire process was just Lee being a thorough physician, really.

Out in the waiting area, Randy continued talking, voice lower but still coming through the intercom perfectly. He'd circled back to his original bragging, as she suspected he eventually would do. "Yeah, this is great news. We're so close, I can almost taste it."

Lee picked up a scrap piece of paper and a pen.

Chapter Nineteen

WE WERE DONE anyway.

Biggest understatement Mav had ever spoken.

His throat burned and shoulders ached as the implications of this entire weekend bore down on him. Soon, he would have nothing left except the dogs. He patted Kenai's head as she and the others lapped up fresh water.

If he lost the lodge, he wouldn't have a place to keep his dogs. His gut twisted in a knot.

The family business, his parents' dream, the wild and beautiful land close enough to town to do his job, the place where his dogs lived—all of it would come to an abrupt end.

At least he still had his paramedic job, and it did give him satisfaction to help patients. That work would fill some of the gaping void. Like a single suture holding together a long, deep laceration, it wouldn't be enough, but it would be something.

He checked his watch. 5:20. He needed to start back to the lodge before the weather turned again. He had to feed the team their dinner. He would return to a home he might have just lost. God, what was he going to tell Dee? His gut clenched. He didn't want to add another loss to all that she already dealt with.

Peering out the window across the parking lot, he stared at the red and white EMERGENCY sign. The shapes of the letters wavered in and out of focus as snow gusts blew past.

Speaking of things he had lost. *We were done anyway.*

With a groan, he sat on the concrete floor next to the team. The sounds of wet lapping and snuffling normally made him smile. He dropped his chin on his knee and watched water dribble out of Bob's lopsided mouth.

Lee made him smile and so much more.

What he'd give to stay in that moment before the satellite phone call.

He loved that Lee wore too many layers because she had no clue how to dress for Alaskan weather. He loved the care she provided the patients in the hospital, treating them all like family. He loved her laughter, enthusiasm, and bright conversation as they hiked with the dogs across the meadow. He loved that she loved his dogs.

He would carry the sensation of her soft lips pressed to his and the feel of her body trembling beneath him for the rest of his life.

Damn it. He dropped a gloved fist on the floor with a muffled *thud*.

Kenai met his gaze with a dog smile filled with trust and love. Like she knew he would take care of them.

He sat up straighter.

No. This couldn't be the end. He would fight. He would challenge whatever litigation Randy planned, right down to Mav's last breath and dollar. The guy was slimy, and Mav was determined to prove it.

Mav might be tired and bruised by his situation, but he didn't want to give up. His dogs needed a home. He would figure out a way to salvage this situation and save his family home. He needed to get back up for himself.

He wanted another chance at something more with Lee.

With what money would he fight?

Damn it, Mav wished he'd never met that guy.

He could start over elsewhere. A bone-deep weariness pressed on him, like gravity exerted twice as much force.

Of course he could start over. It was always an option. He wasn't without skills. He could go to Fairbanks where a paramedic salary covered a small house or an apartment in town. He could sign on with the LifeMed flight team out of Fairbanks. In the past, they'd offered him a position, with a signing bonus.

None of that gave him what he wanted—the dogs, the lodge, a business to build, hanging out with Dee, his life in Yukon Valley.

And Lee.

The realization hit him like a punch to the gut. Lee held a piece of his heart. She was important to Mav.

Damn it, the timing sucked. He couldn't act on his feelings. What was he supposed to say? *Hey, I recently lost everything and have a limited future source of income and might be homeless and besides you'll be leaving soon, want to hang out?*

It wasn't about money. Sure, he understood that she earned more than him. That fact didn't make him insecure. In a relationship, he felt confident when he stood on his own two feet and made a meaningful contribution. Food, shelter, safety, shared interests, effort, support.

He wanted a partnership. He'd glimpsed the possibility in Lee's intelligent brown eyes when they talked and when they worked together to take care of patients.

What he had wanted had been *right there*. Exhaustion wormed its way through him.

With one last pet of Kenai's head, he collected the dogs' bowls and thanked Louise and Hilda. He couldn't fix his life right now, but he could care for his dogs.

Time to get back on the trail, feed them, and get the babies safely settled in at home ... for as long as home lasted.

Kenai pressed her head against his knee and looked up at him with soulful eyes. She trusted that he'd take care of her.

Mav prepared to fight.

Chapter Twenty

LEE ROLLED OVER in the hospital call room Sunday morning and stretched her sore muscles with a groan. Yesterday's hiking with dogs—or rather, dogs pulling hiker—and taking care of Nick with his accident had worn her out. After casting Nick's leg and discharging him, Lee spent more than an hour carefully reviewing her chart note.

That one document could make or break several people's futures.

At least her extra work last night meant she could add some billable hours for her locums timesheet. For Lee, every dollar mattered these days.

Sighing, she sat up and squinted at her cell phone, bright in the dark call room. A red dot popped up, indicating a message. Her heart sped up, then dropped.

It wasn't Maverick. Nothing from him.

It gave her emotional whiplash, how they had gone from mutual heavy petting that was likely leading to something even sexier, to disaster then despair in a matter of hours. Lee wished she could give Maverick a big hug right now, even if he didn't feel that he could reciprocate.

Man, Lee hated bullies.

She rubbed her face and tapped the screen. The message

177

was from the locums company recruiter. Unusual to have a message come in—she checked the timestamp—an hour ago. Recruiters generally didn't work on weekends unless there was an urgent reason.

She sat back on the pillows and read the message.

Emergency request for a three-month assignment in southern Utah. You would be the only doc covering the facility for half of that time. Hospital is willing to pay double your current assignment fees and will buy out the remainder of Alaska assignment if you will transfer before your assignment ends there. Details in email sent to you.

Lee quickly did some math and leaned back on the bed. *Oh wow.*

Hadn't she worried about her bank account and the immediate need to clear multiple debts?

Hadn't she complained about how bitterly cold it was here?

Hadn't she deflected staff members' gentle comments about her remaining in Yukon Valley?

The planned completion date of her assignment was the end of March. Right now, it was the first week of February.

Her thoughts whirled.

Yukon Valley needed her until Dr. Pitka returned from maternity leave.

Lee's job as a locums doc was to help staff facilities so that patients would receive safe, high-quality care in situations where the local docs were overextended or services had to divert because there weren't enough doctors.

Of course, that was the reason on paper.

But she chose locums work for the quick fix on her finances, too. Her goal had been to go to wherever paid the most. Get back on her feet as fast as possible.

Take the offer from the highest bidder and help a hospital in dire need. Everyone wins.

Right?

She glanced at the time. Eight a.m. Barely enough time to shower and meet Deirdre, who had offered to swing her by the lodge this morning so Lee could pick up her car.

While there, Lee would check on Nick. Maybe Maverick, too.

What would he say to her?

Southern Utah. She rolled the location around in her mind. Warmer. Rural but less isolated than Yukon Valley. More lucrative.

What would she tell Maverick?

If she moved forward with the assignment, it wouldn't matter what she said to him. She pressed a palm to her aching chest, unable to make a decision.

She was *not* in a headspace to evaluate the offer right now. Best to give it a little time and think things through.

Rushing to get ready, she tried to ignore the recruiter's message. She also ignored things like feelings and what-ifs and credit card bills. All of it could wait until tomorrow.

Twenty minutes later, she closed Deirdre's Subaru door and buckled up. "Thanks for giving me a ride this morning." Lee was back in her outdoor gear from yesterday's rescue.

Deirdre pulled away from the hospital. "Not a problem. Phew, what a crazy night."

True. Not only had Lee wrapped up Nick's ER care, but

then she had helped with the C-section and resuscitated the baby. When it was all done, everyone was healthy. Without keys to the rental house or transportation, it had been easier to stay in the hospital.

Biting her lip, Lee said, "Didn't expect quite this much adventure when I signed up to work in Yukon Valley."

"Sounds like adventure found you."

"That's a good way to put it." She smiled, but it felt tight, like a grimace instead.

After a moment, Deirdre shifted, her coat material *shushing* in the close quarters. "Can I mention something?"

"Sure."

"I'm really glad you're here. Not only for the medical part—everyone appreciates your care. I know Dr. Moore and Dr. Burmeister and Dr. Pitka are so glad you're part of the team. I'm sure someone has offered this, but we would love to have you continue working here at Yukon Valley. Indefinitely."

Lee made a noncommittal, vaguely positive sound.

Planting her mittened hands on the wheel at ten and two to navigate the snowy ruts leading from this side street to the main highway, Deirdre continued, "But on a personal level, you're a friend."

"I agree."

She paused for a few seconds. "I'm also glad for what you've done for Mav."

Lee's head whipped over. "What?" How did she know? Had she read the chart notes? Lee hadn't told anyone about the extent of her notes and the reasons why she'd documented in that manner. Terrified of giving up protected patient information, she clamped her mouth shut.

Deirdre didn't seem to notice Lee's distress. "He might be my younger brother and a royal pain in the patoots, but I care about him and want him to be happy. He's smiled more in the past month than in the past two years."

"Oh. Mm-hmm." She unclenched her hands. After a moment, she managed to say, "It's easy for anyone to smile when you live in a beautiful lodge at the edge of gorgeous wilderness."

Deirdre glanced over out the corner of her eye. "What about the dogs?"

"They're adorable!"

"I know. I don't get to spend nearly enough time with them." She sighed. "After our parents died, Mav and I have struggled to keep the mortgage above water. That ship seems to be sinking."

"Hmm."

"He's always wanted to develop Mom and Dad's property into an all-season wilderness destination."

"You both own it."

"It's important to me, but not like it is for Mav." She flicked the turn signal to turn right onto the state highway. "He was worried about this weekend. Felt like a lot was riding on the exposure this trip might provide."

This morning, Lee had seen the latest Yelp review for Maverick's business, and it wasn't complimentary. Of course, there was no mention about the role the review's author, Randy, had in his own bad decision-making. The review had been cross-posted to several social media sites. How could someone fight slander when people were entitled to their opinion, no matter how ill-informed?

"Exposure." Lee tapped her mittened fingers on the door's armrest. "Posting."

"Yes, reviews, referring friends."

"Word of mouth. Rumors going across town and back," she murmured. "'More connections on social media than the national power grid has outlets.'" Like her colleague Kathy had said. Lee sat up straight. "Any chance we could stop at Three Bears?"

"Sure." Deirdre flicked the turn signal the other way and made a left on the highway, then a right into the Three Bears parking lot.

"I won't be but a minute. Thanks!" Lee ducked into the store, hoping that Tuli was working the Sunday morning shift. Weaving her way through the array of office supplies, children's clothing, and food products, she followed her nose to the smoked meats in the back.

Empty.

"Shoot."

A few seconds later, a head popped out from the back room. "Hi, Doc!" he said with a broad smile.

"Tuli, I'm glad you're here." Suddenly, nerves fluttered in her stomach. Would Maverick understand what she was doing and why? Would it make a difference?

"What can I get you? Sliced meat? Ground chuck?"

An impulse to retreat and quit this stupid plan made her leg muscles tense, but she planted her feet. "I need something that's not found in the deli, but I believe is your area of expertise."

He leaned on the counter, chin propped on his fists. "You have my attention."

Chapter Twenty-One

MAV DRAGGED HIS sorry butt out of bed early Sunday to check on the babies and feed them breakfast. None of them were the worse for wear, despite yesterday's impromptu runs without correctly timing their nutrition.

He didn't need an alarm clock this morning.

He hadn't slept since he and the team had arrived back at the lodge yesterday evening.

He had waited up until one of the guests returned in the SUV with Nick and Randy.

Nick had clomped through the great room on crutches with a fiberglass cast on his leg, thanks to the *pretty Dr. Tipton*. He seemed slightly woozy but comfortable, which was a decent outcome, all things considered.

Now Mav stood in his wool socks, outdoor pants, and a dark blue flannel shirt as he cooked up Sunday morning breakfast. Hey, the guests had reserved the bed and breakfast plan, and no way would Mav shirk his duties, despite everything that had happened. Reputation mattered, even in a crappy situation. He knew that from EMS work. His parents had ingrained in him the integrity to carry out his commitments in a professional manner.

No matter how rude the customer.

Mav laid sizzling caribou sausages on a plate and grabbed a piece to chew while he cooked more links. He peered out the kitchen window at the faint dawn glow on orange clouds between the spruce pines. He memorized the view, like he might not see it again.

Yukon Valley was so far off the beaten path, there *was* no beaten path. Online direction apps basically took one look at any Yukon Valley address and went *good luck*. A few miles west of town, the highway simply stopped. Only endless bush and miles of river beyond that point.

Nothing was out here except for the lodge and cabins, a small town and a few villages, sled and snowmobile trails, and millions of acres of mountain and snowy tundra wilderness, which he loved exploring with his team.

He'd better enjoy it while he could.

The sausage sat like a hot coal in his gut. He took a swig of orange juice with minimal improvement. Between his gritty eyelids, tired muscles, and complete lack of sleep, Mav was as wrung out as that worn dishtowel hanging over the sink faucet.

At least Lee hadn't returned last night. Dee had texted to let him know she was dropping Lee off at the lodge to get her car this morning. Hopefully, she'd miss the guests. Hey, he was man enough to own up to his failures and limitations, but that didn't mean he wanted someone he cared about to witness his last pathetic stand.

At nine a.m. sharp, the cabin guests entered through the front door, joined shortly by Randy and then by Nick crutching along from the guest rooms. Mav gamely served up the full breakfast spread—caribou sausage, salmon cakes, seasoned fried potatoes, stewed tomatoes, sourdough French bread with birch syrup and salmonberry preserves, orange juice, and coffee. The guests continued talking about their travel back to Fairbanks today and then Randy going to Anchorage tomorrow.

Leaving a day early, thanks to the accident. Mav would refund them the extra night. Damn it. He had needed the income.

A few minutes later, his sister and Lee came through the front door, peeling off coats, gloves, and boots in the entryway. He appreciated the leggings that hugged Lee's curves.

"Hey, our waitress service arrived." Randy laughed, the other men joining him.

Dee strolled up to the table and glowered at him until he turned red. God, his sister was terrifying.

Randy raised his hands, a fork held in one. "It's a joke, lady. Take it easy."

She slid her gaze to Mav and raised her eyebrows. He had updated her as to what had happened last night, so she knew the basic story and the main actors.

He shook his head, and she clamped her lips together.

Just because she knew the situation didn't make her any less likely to take a swipe at Randy.

"Oh, and your *friend* is back, too." Randy clearly enjoyed being the gregarious center of attention. "Didn't realize she was that pretty under all the clothes yesterday."

Mav wanted to cram the spatula down the man's throat.

Lee's long gold hair was on glorious display this morning.

She grimaced. "Glad everyone is safe and sound."

When Nick saw her, he did a double take. "You look like the doctor from last night. I think. It's all a little fuzzy. I don't think she had blond hair."

"Naw, this gal's an EMT. Works with him," Randy butted in. "You're confused from those knockout drugs they gave you."

Lee's eyes narrowed, but she pasted on a bland, polite smile and made a noncommittal sound as she followed Dee into the kitchen. Mav didn't know which woman would eviscerate Randy, but the sooner the better.

Randy wiped his face on the napkin, wadded it up next to his plate, and leaned back in the chair. "I like this dining area and kitchen, but it needs some spiffing up. Maybe an addition or a redo of the layout. Knock out a wall or two. Modernize."

Mav's ears rang, but he refused to take the bait. He joined his sister and Lee near the sink. "Counting down the minutes until they leave," he muttered.

"I can make that time go faster." Dee's savage smile did not bode well for anyone.

"Boys, what do you think about this place? I'm buying it. All of it," Randy said loudly.

Murmurs, congratulations, and confused expressions circled the table.

Mav spun around. "What?" He glanced at the desk drawer stuffed with past-due notices and offers to purchase.

The clues began to fall into place.

Next to him, Lee didn't move.

"Getting it for a song, once the bank finishes their work," Randy continued.

Dee clanked a plate in the sink. Hard. "That's it, I'm going in."

Mav grabbed his sister but missed Lee, who sauntered to the table. "How do you figure that?" Her Southern accent thickened into a sweet, charming voice that snagged everyone's attention.

"You don't know? Your boyfriend here is broke. The business will be belly-up after I post more customer reviews of the unsafe equipment and trails out here. Also, my nephew here is going to sue."

Nick kept his eyes on his plate.

"Why would he sue?" Lee said.

Randy gave her a broad, patronizing smile. "That wreck was the owner's fault, sweetheart. Faulty machine. Poor maintenance. Trails are dangerous."

"You did sign a waiver," Mav growled, standing next to her.

He shrugged. "We'll tie you up in court and publicize it. There won't be anything left of this place once foreclosure hits. Nothing left." He grinned. "Except for gold."

"Huh?" Mav shook his head and looked at Dee, who shrugged.

"This property sits on a vein of gold. This location is at the tail end of the Ray Mountains. A survey fifty years ago listed this as proven and probable resource, not only for gold but also some rare earth elements that are currently in high demand."

Dee removed some of the men's empty dishes. "No seriously, what are you talking about?" She turned to Mav. "Mom and Dad never mentioned anything about mining."

"She's your sister? Oh, that's rich. Get it? Rich." Randy laughed at his joke and speared a piece of caribou, chewed, and swallowed. "About ten years ago, I was poking around in the public USGS records down in the Seattle office searching for speculation properties and came across the survey for this parcel. It had been misfiled, so no one knew it existed. I had been in the process of getting an updated survey— contingent before I made the purchase. That's when your folks swooped in before I could complete the survey and stole the property out from under me."

Mav opened his mouth but nothing came out.

Dee's expression matched his.

A thrumming pulse in Mav's forehead momentarily blocked out sound. He and his sister were about to lose far more than anyone had realized. He stared at the desk with the letters and the BLM and USGS mail. His fingers itched to open those envelopes right now.

With a warm smile, Lee walked around the table next to Randy. "So, wait. All you have to do is get the bank to foreclose, and you get the property?"

"Yep. Bank has my paperwork ready to go."

"What's to keep someone else from buying it first?"

He grinned. "I'm friends with the president of the bank that holds this property's mortgage. First in line." He rested his elbows on the table. "To make sure the foreclosure happens quickly, Nick's going to sue for damages and negligence."

She nodded. "Oh, so that will speed up the part where they can't pay the mortgage. By chewing up their resources in legal fees and attorneys or tanking the business."

"You got it."

"To make them use up their money, Nick is going to sue." She tapped a finger on her full lower lip.

Mav shifted from foot to foot, squirming at the way Lee laid out what was going to happen. Didn't matter how, Mav would fight Randy to the end.

"As well he should," Randy said. "I mean, look at him with the broken leg and all."

He seemed fine to Mav, except for the injury, which, by the way, was covered by liability waivers and business insurance. His face grew hot.

Almost to herself, she said, "You'll need the medical notes to support the claim."

He bristled. "Obviously, sweetheart. Once the lawyers see the report, we can decide how many zeros to put on the settlement."

Mav could swear that Lee clamped her lips together for a beat. Then she probed, "Or?" His satisfied grin split his face. "Or we go to court, which costs time and money he doesn't have, on account of his failing business."

"Failing business. You'll ensure that everyone knows?" Lee's logic knifed right through Mav.

"I mean, I can't control who sees what in online reviews

and social media posts." Randy spoke slowly, like explaining something to a child.

Mav rolled his hands into fists, tense but resisting the real desire to cram his knuckles into the guy.

Randy continued. "Well, here's the fun part. We don't have to win the lawsuit. We just need to drag it out long enough for funds to run out so they can't make payments and for the bank to foreclose."

Mav gritted his teeth and again stepped up next to her, like he craved proximity.

Lee pursed her lips and scanned Dee and Mav, then Randy. "You need the doctor's report to prove your case. Seal the deal."

"Are you slow?" His brows drew together.

Mav stepped forward, ready to rearrange the guy's features for insulting Lee.

She rested her fingertips on his arm and continued, "Wonder what that doctor's report says. Don't you?" She ignored whatever Randy mumbled and turned to Nick. "You signed up for the patient portal on the electronic medical records, right?"

"Think so. The checkout person gave me the info to download the app," Nick said, picking up his phone and tapping. "Is the note there already?"

"Should be. There's a new federal rule regarding notes being immediately available to patients."

Randy gaped at her. "How do you know that?"

Lee didn't answer him. "Hey, Nick, can you pull up that note?" She smiled at him and batted her eyes. "I want to see how bad things will be when the judge reads the note, don't you?"

Mav's heart pounded. His head spun. What was she doing? Pouring virtual gasoline on the place and then lighting a match?

"Um." Nick was putty in her hands. "Yeah. Okay." He beamed up at her.

Sauntering over, she lightly touched Nick's shoulder. "Oh wow. Look at that, you've got the app running and everything." She fawned over him. "You mind reading the first section of that note? I'd like to see if it's as good as Randy's hoping." Her words came out slower, softer, the syllables drawn out.

Mav bristled, then recalled their conversation a few weeks ago. *The worse the situation gets, the slower I talk.*

"Uh, sure." Nick scrolled.

Randy leaned back, arms over his chest.

No one in the room made a sound.

Nick read, "'Patient states that he was on a trail near a vacation lodge when he hit a bump and flew off the snowmachine, injuring his leg. He states he does not believe he struck his head. Witnesses present do not report that he had loss of consciousness. He is not complaining of pain in any other areas besides the leg. Denies chest pain, shortness of breath, cough, dizziness, headache, difficulty moving his neck or noninjured extremities.'"

Randy nodded with a smile.

Dee and Mav hadn't moved. Hearing this report was like the reading of a last will and testament. Only, no one got anything. Except for Randy.

Nick looked up at Lee, who indicated for him to continue. "'Per witnesses and first responders to the scene, no mental status changes were noted before, during, and after the accident. Per first responders, no neck pain, spine pain, or spine deformity was noted in the field. Patient was transported to the ED with appropriate precautions. In the ED patient denies use of drugs or alcohol. Patient states that his uncle, Randy, who was present at the accident, had hoped to fabricate an injury so that he could sue the lodge owner. Patient states that Randy had not planned for the injury to be severe. Patient states that he is in pain relative to his leg injury. His pain has improved with morphine, which was given upon arrival to the ED.'"

"What." Blotches of red crept up Randy's face as he spluttered. "That's enough," he said.

"Read on." Lee crossed her arms.

"We're done here." Randy made to stand up, but Mav stepped forward and glared him into place.

"Nope. Read," Lee said.

Nick glanced at her warily but complied. "'Patient could not tolerate entering the CT scanner without sedation. Versed two milligrams IV given prior to imaging.'" He swallowed. "'Patient's history was taken at bedside with nurse A.J. present.'"

Mav froze. Amberlyn Jenkins. Damn. Lee had a witness to the statements.

"Uncle Randy, I don't remember this."

Lee patted Nick on the shoulder, then strolled around

the table. "Versed is one of my favorite antianxiety medications that I regularly use. In my job. As a doctor. At this hospital."

One of the men mumbled, "Oh crap." He elbowed the guy next to him.

Mav watched the scene, riveted.

"Versed is helpful for anxiety, but it has an interesting property of disinhibiting people. There are studies about using it as a truth serum. Not sure if it's really good for that or not. I find that it makes people ... comfortable and chatty."

"You drugged him for information?" Randy spluttered. "That's illegal. You could be sued."

Lee pivoted, her voice ice-cold and clinical. "No. The attending physician—that's me—treated his anxiety with standard use of an FDA-approved medication so that the appropriate tests could be performed. I documented his history of present illness in the medical record. It's literally my job to do those things."

Randy gaped like a salmon on dry land. "This is all hearsay. Coercion. You led him."

"I can see how someone might think that." She took another step then pivoted to face him a few feet away. She was like a spider spinning a web for Randy to wander into. "That's why I added more medically pertinent information to the record. Nick, could you read the next paragraph?"

There was more? Mav didn't dare move.

Nick cleared his throat. "'This writer observed a person identified as patient's uncle Randy speaking on the phone in the waiting room. He was heard stating that *This accident was exactly what I need to run that business into the ground.* He stated that *He wasn't supposed to break his leg, but it's a bonus.*'" Nick stared at his uncle but kept reading, eyes wide. "'He stated that he had the bank contact ready to send him the papers to sign as soon as the lawsuit is settled and foreclosure begins.'" He swallowed. "I got a broken leg for nothing, Uncle Randy?"

Mav stepped up and slung an arm around Lee. Her chin was lifted, and her gaze remained steady and narrowed, but she trembled.

What an amazing woman. He squeezed her shoulder.

"That's—that's one of those HIPAA violations, lady," Randy spat. "You shared his medical information without his permission. We will report you to the medical board."

Lee took a solid five seconds before answering, all syrupy-sweet with a gracious, pitying smile. "Bless your heart, Randy. Today is your lucky day. As it turns out, I'm an expert on patient privacy law. It's not a HIPAA violation if the patient is the one who freely shares their health information with others. Besides, this information would have come out eventually. What do you know? I just saved you a bunch of money in attorney fees. You are very welcome."

Sweat beaded Randy's forehead.

"Also …" She paused. "Are any of you lawyers by any chance? No? Because I could be wrong, but I believe your hosts have a case for personal fraud and libel. There might even be a case for insurance fraud."

Mav rocked back on his heels. He stood up straighter

and squared his shoulders.

Lee had put on a masterclass in weaponizing Southern charm and healthcare regulation.

The only sound was Kenai's faint snore in the other room.

Mav kept his arm tightly around Lee. "Gentlemen"—the term was being used loosely and with dripping sarcasm— "you'll understand if I ask you to pack up and leave. Right now."

The mutters of befuddled and angry guests rose as they scraped chairs back.

"Y'all come back now, you hear?" Lee waggled her fingers.

Chapter Twenty-Two

"ARE YOU KIDDING me?" Maverick spun Lee around and kissed her until she couldn't breathe.

He hadn't shaved since yesterday, and the bristles tickled.

Laughing, she threw her arms around his neck. "I hate bullies." She stepped away and held out her hands, still shaking.

Deirdre raised her arms. "My turn." A quick hug and she grinned. "That was so beautifully passive-aggressive, it brought a tear to my eye."

"Killing them with kindness and medical documentation." Lee batted her eyes.

Maverick stared at Lee. "I can't believe you did that. All of it."

"I was in the right place at the right time with the right skill set. Besides, I couldn't sit around and let them steal your family's place."

"You're amazing." His blue gaze locked on to hers.

Her neck warmed up. "Welp."

Another few seconds passed.

Deirdre broke the awkward silence. "*Welp* is right." She pointed with both thumbs toward the front of the house, where slams of car doors and tones of low voices filtered over. With a thoughtful expression and raised brows, his sister studied Lee and Maverick until Lee started to squirm. "Hmm. So. All righty, then. I'm heading out. See you two later this week?"

"Yes!" they both said.

She pulled on boots, grabbed her coat, and swept out the door, whistling a happy tune.

Maverick cupped Lee's face as he leaned in for another kiss that went on and on until her toes tingled. She inhaled the fresh air and spruce scent that was uniquely his. He kept kissing her.

Until the sound of tromping boots and crutches across the great room floor behind them broke the moment.

Maverick growled, tucked Lee in to his side, and turned. "Need help with luggage?" he asked.

Randy and Nick grunted. The front door slammed shut.

Maverick shot her a sideways grin. "Guessing that's a *no*."

A few seconds later, Lee started to shake in earnest.

"Are you okay?" He pulled out two dining table chairs to face each other and helped her sit in one of them.

She scrubbed her palms over her face. "Shoo wee. I'm not the confrontational type. That was nerve-racking."

"That was remarkable."

Dropping her hands, she laughed nervously. "I can't believe how everything went down."

He pressed her cold hands between his warm ones. His flannel button-down shirtsleeves were rolled up, showing his corded forearms, dusted in light brown hair. "Thank you. I mean it. You took a professional risk to help."

For a minute there, nothing had mattered to Lee other than doing the right thing here in Yukon Valley. Blinking hard, Lee said, "All's well that ends well."

"Well, partly." His brows pulled together. "Randy better not poke his head into our business again. But what's to stop someone else doing the same thing? The issue is payments to the bank. We have to meet our obligations with revenue."

"How?"

"Bookings. Word of mouth. Good reviews." He kissed her fingertips and studied their joined hands. "Which we won't get from this last crew."

The brush of his lips sent a frisson of pleasure into her chest. "How do you know?"

"Know what?"

"Whether you have a booking?"

"Huh? Well, the website is linked to our reservations software. There was nothing scheduled as of yesterday night."

"Check again. You never know." She prayed Tuli had worked his magic as quickly as he'd promised.

"Lee. Come on, now. We won this battle with Randy. Everything else is wishful thinking." With a shake of his head, he pulled out his phone and opened an app. "Okay." He tapped. Frowned. Scrolled up and down. Rubbed his chin. "What the hell?"

"What?"

"We set our available dates a year in advance, based on my schedule and Dee's. Between the two of us, we can free up nine or ten days a month." He stared at the screen. "I don't understand. We're fifty percent booked through June." He scrolled again. "Wait. Fall hunting season already has reservations."

"That's good."

"Hell yes, that's good. That's income we can plan on." He put the phone on the table. "How? You did this, too?"

"Nope." She shook her head. "Tuli." Craving the contact, she pulled his hand to her cheek. "He's a social media influencer who runs the popular The Real Alaska account, apparently. Lots of connections. And he's your friend."

"Why?"

"Why is he your friend or why did he do this?"

Maverick's stunned expression resembled someone who'd been hit by a two-by-four upside the head. "The second one."

"I mentioned to him that some exposure might help counteract the incoming jerk reviews."

"That's it?"

"Basically." She paused. "He started mumbling about cross-promoting and calling in favors with influencer friends and ran with it, I guess."

"Huh." His brows furrowed. "Should've thought of asking him a long time ago."

"You were busy with an entire business plus running Yukon Valley's EMS department. No time to refine marketing strategy."

He looked back down at the phone. "Wow."

"Also …" She hesitated. It hurt to say the words. "I do

understand what it feels like to have a bully take things away. To stand on shaky financial ground and wonder what the future holds. I get it." With a whisper, she confessed aloud her embarrassment. "I'm there right now. With nothing."

"Lee." He drew her hand up to brush his lips across her wrist. "After what you've done for my sister and for me, I want to help with your situation."

For several seconds longer than she cared to say, Lee considered it. Thought about a future in Yukon Valley and out of the financial hole she'd landed in. Thought about what gold and other ore could mean in terms of money. Then she studied Maverick's handsome, open expression. "I can't accept the help. It's tempting, but I need to do this myself. For myself."

His blue gaze held hers. "I get it. You will get back on your feet, I bet sooner than you think."

Inwardly, she flinched. He was way too close to the truth. "Sure hope so. For both of us."

With the pads of his thumbs, he lightly rubbed the backs of her hands. Little sparks of heat zipped up her arms at the simple touch. He closed the short distance between them and dropped a gentle kiss on her mouth as he slid his hands into her hair.

"Mm, feels so good to touch you." His voice had dropped an octave.

At the sensual tone, heat coiled low in her pelvis. "What now?" she said after another kiss.

He pulled her straight onto his lap, holding her loosely at the hips as he kissed her again. When he curled two corded arms around her back and pressed her into his chest, all of her nerve endings lit up like a Christmas tree. Lee looped her arms around his neck and relaxed into him.

"What now?" he repeated the question in between brushes of his mouth over hers. "No guests."

"Hang out with the babies?" Her heart scampered as he traced the tip of his tongue over her lips.

"I love the babies, but they're not you," he murmured against her mouth. "Hate to miss out on a window of opportunity where both of our schedules line up."

"Do tell."

He pulled back, his breath feathering the hair around her face. "I want to continue what we started yesterday. This time without distractions. Any distractions. I want to give you my complete attention." The way he said the word *complete* made it sound like a promise and a sensual challenge.

"Oh?" *Oh yes*, more like it.

"If that's what you'd like." His pupils had dilated to the point where only a rim of blue remained.

She shifted on his lap, trying and failing to douse the heat building in her core. Now wasn't the time for career decisions or an existential evaluation. Now was the time for more kisses. "I'd love that." He rolled his hips against her, and she gasped. "I'd love all of that."

His steady gaze met hers as he stood with her in his arms, grasping under her thighs. Lee wrapped her legs around his waist and tightened the grip of her hands behind his neck. Muscles bunched as he carried her across the room. He toed open the door to the master bedroom and gently sat her on the bed.

Like she was as delicate as a snowflake.

She was not. Lee was as tough as one of those icicles hanging from the eaves, formed in harsh conditions over time.

This icicle deserved to melt a little.

Lee licked her lips and grabbed the front of his flannel shirt, throwing him off-balance. They tumbled back onto the bed.

He landed on top of her and scooted her up the mattress, kissing her neck. His fingers spearing into her hair felt like heaven on her scalp.

Their harsh breaths filled the quiet room. Rasps of her fingertips on his unshaved jaw punctuated the wet slide of their mouths together. She loved his growling hunger and the cords of his arms flexing as he leaned over her.

More. Lee wanted more.

She wanted to feel cherished and valued.

She needed to trust this moment and trust her heart.

She deserved pleasure and passion, given by a rugged Alaskan man who was as breathtaking as the wild landscape he lived in.

Above everything else, right this minute, she wanted more of the hot, sexy sensations waking up nerve endings that had slept for years, maybe longer.

Lee wanted Maverick. She fumbled at the buttons on his shirt.

With a big grin, he sat up, unbuttoned the top two buttons, and pulled off the flannel and T-shirt beneath in one delicious motion that flexed muscles of his chest and arms. Light brown hair dusted his skin.

She trailed fingers across a pectoralis and then drifted lower over his abdominals, drawing out a shudder.

Maverick grabbed her wrists. "You're going to make me lose my mind."

"That's the idea."

"I want that job."

"You already have two jobs."

"Yeah, but this makes for a hell of a side gig." He smoothed his hands under her thermal top until a soft hiss came from her lips. "May I?"

"Does a sled dog like snow?"

Laughing, he helped her sit up long enough to slip the thermal shirt off and remove her bra. The air cooled her hot skin.

Then his hands were everywhere. On her neck, her face, in her hair, drifting down her side, palming her breasts. He rocked his pants-clad hardness into her pelvis and laced her fingers in his above her head.

Then he dipped down to suck one nipple into his mouth, laving the tip with his rough tongue. He gave a gentle bite, and her hips bucked under him. Still sucking her nipple, he lifted up and released her with a wet pop. With a broad smile, he turned his attention to the other breast.

His knees tightened around her hips, holding her thighs together, adding pressure to her core.

"Off," she said.

He frowned and stopped what he was doing. "You want me off of you?"

"No. Pants. Off." She gasped.

"Well, if it's doctor's orders ..." He unbuckled the belt, undid a button, and pulled the zipper down, each metallic tick ricocheting a new shiver down her spine. Then he stopped and shot her a sly smile. "However. Fair's fair."

"What? Ohhh."

In a flurry of movement, he lifted her hips and slid the rest of her clothes off, until all she had on were her wool socks.

"It's cool in here," he said. "Want to keep the socks on?"

She sat up and smoothed her hands over his tight glutes that were exposed by the loose waistband. "Do you care?" Tugging his pants down, she reached inside the garment.

His gaze swept over her body. "Not one bit. I was think—"

He bit off the word as she wrapped her fingers around his hard erection. In a split second, Maverick was completely naked, with a condom in his hand and a grin on his face.

He set the condom on the mattress next to her, like a promise about to be fulfilled. Her heart rate sped up. Leaning down, he kissed his way across her abdomen, over her thighs, and back up, stopping short of the heated area that ached for him. Goosebumps followed the trail of his mouth. Restless, unable to find relief, she moved her hips.

His mouth was so close.

A tiny moan slipped out between her lips.

"Would you like to make a suggestion?" He chuckled,

watching her from half-mast eyelids as he knelt between her knees.

"More. Please." She gasped, fisting the bedding near her hip.

Time slowed down as he watched her from where he rested, poised at the juncture of her thighs.

He reached up to meet her hand and laced their fingers together once more.

Then he ducked his head and swept his tongue over her hot flesh.

"Oh my God." Her lower back arched off the bed with the first lick.

Maverick squeezed her hand and continued to slide his mouth over her, dipping into her core, sliding along the sensitive area between her labia, then back up to stroke her clitoris with the flat of his tongue. She flew along with hisses of air through her pursed lips, bliss dimming the edges of her vision.

He lifted his head and made eye contact. Moisture glistened on his mouth.

Placing two fingers in his mouth, he watched her.

Lee didn't look away.

His neck and jaw muscles rippled.

Her core pulsed, hips rocking toward him, needing to feel him inside of her, needing … Maverick.

He pulled his fingers out and slid them home in her vagina.

A shower of sparks cascaded through her. "Maverick, I— Please. I need—"

He didn't move his hand.

Lee pressed her hips up, craving more, wanting to feel movement. He released their clasped fingers and palmed her thigh. Then he gave a sucking lick over her sensitive flesh at the same time as he drew his fingers in and out, the rhythm slowly speeding up, driving her higher and higher.

Lee grabbed the blanket and rode the sensations coiling deep inside of her. He curled his fingers with a strong, sure movement as he flicked his tongue over her clitoris.

Her world exploded in blissful sound and light and sensation as she tightened over and against his fingers for what seemed like hours. Were those her wild cries? Every nerve ending buzzed to life, and she floated on wave after wave of aftershocks until she finally relaxed.

"Oh my God, Maverick."

"Lee, you are amazing."

Chapter Twenty-Three

THE SCENT OF Lee's desire would be imprinted on Mav's brain until the end of time. Musky and sweet. He wanted to lose himself in her. Taste her until she came apart in his arms over and over.

His dick, however, had other plans. Pressure mounted.

He sat up, loving how her splayed legs exposed her glistening folds. He loved her eyes, half-lidded from pleasure. Her pebbled nipples tempted him to lick and nip. A flush tinted her upper chest and neck. This was all his doing, and he felt darn proud for it.

"Maverick," she murmured.

"Yeah, Lee?"

"I want you inside of me."

He could sightsee later. "Don't need to ask me twice."

Quickly, he rolled the condom over his pulsing erection and nudged at her entrance, teasing both of them. They groaned in unison, anticipation ratcheting up the tension.

Sliding an arm under her knee, he knelt and thrust into her sweet, slick heat. He let go of her leg, leaned over, and kissed her.

Lee locked her ankles behind him, wool-sock-covered heels digging into his butt, and he plunged into her harder and faster, their gasps and cries blending together.

Mav lifted her hips, giving him a better angle, and rocked into her with deep looping strokes. He leaned over again and pressed his forehead to hers as the tension rose to a breaking point. Driving in faster, he sensed her inner muscles flutter around him, then clench in a perfect rhythm, and he shouted her name as he came apart inside of her.

WHEN MAV LANDED back down on Earth, he couldn't move. Every bone in his body had turned to rubber. Was he crushing Lee?

She rubbed her palms along his back with a satisfied hum and wiggled her hips, sending ricochets of aftershocks through him.

"Mmm," she said, meeting his lips in a deep kiss. "That was wonderful."

"You're wonderful." He brushed his lips over her forehead. "Hold that thought."

With reluctance, he eased out of her and hurried to the bathroom to clean up. He returned to the bed where she had already burrowed under the blankets, and he slid in behind her, snugging her body up against him.

"Lee." His heart pounded and his mouth went dry.

"Yes."

He nuzzled the skin under her ear until she shivered against him. "I might be falling in love with you."

Lee rolled toward him, staying within the circle of his

arms. "I was thinking the same thing."

He blinked and swallowed hard. "I know you're here on a temporary basis. I get it, but I want to try and see if something could work out." Confident that his business would survive, he could now envision a future together.

For a few seconds, she stiffened in his arms. "Seems like this is working out fine." She didn't meet his eyes but gave a catlike smile and stretched against him, making them both groan.

Mav noted her tense expression. "You like it enough here?"

"It's different from what I'm used to, but it's a beautiful place. I like what I do. I like the people. And I like you."

He drew his hand down her flushed cheek. "But?"

"There are a lot of things going on personally right now."

"That sounded like a hedge if I've ever heard one." He studied her warm eyes and her kiss-swollen lips. "No pressure for any future."

"No pressure." She repeated his words, but there was a bitter edge to them.

A warmth grew in his chest. "I want to do right by you, Lee."

"That's not an issue." She kissed him, tucked her head into his chest, and snuggled deeper into his arms.

Within a few minutes, she had drifted off to sleep. She might not be at a place where they could discuss long-term plans. He understood. But she hadn't said *never*.

Lee had given him her body and her trust.

Mav would protect that gift with everything he had in the hopes that she might one day give him her heart.

Chapter Twenty-Four

LEE'S HEAD ITCHED with the eerie feeling that someone was watching her. She opened one eye.

A gray muzzle and two soulful eyes peered at her over the edge of the bed. Kenai sat with her chin propped on the mattress.

She leaned over and petted the dog. "You're a sweetie." Rolling onto her back, she felt the mattress next to her. A slight warmth remained, which meant Maverick had been up for a while.

Light filtered into the bedroom. Still daylight. Hard to tell the exact time. She turned and glanced at the bedside clock. 1:50 p.m. Wow, she'd slept that long?

Taking jerks down a peg must have knocked the stuffing out of her.

No, amazing sex with a rugged Alaskan had worn her out. She'd gladly do it again. Lee stretched with a satisfied groan. The soreness in her hips reminded her of each skin-to-skin moment with Maverick.

Was this real? She checked in with her innermost self, making sure this wasn't some kind of rebound after her divorce. A reaction. Too soon?

There wasn't a standard amount of time from the end of

one relationship and the beginning of another. Like, *ding*, three months later, good to go. Or six months, or a year. Truth be told, her relationship with Preston was over several years ago.

Her OB fellowship attending had another saying. *Life is what happens when you're making plans.*

Lee had wanted to run away from her life in Georgia. To reorganize her life. To learn to trust herself again. To reset her financial situation and confidently stand on her own two feet, independent and secure in her choices. She had made plans, but in the middle of all of those plans, her life had just … happened.

Yukon Valley with all the challenges of this frontier hospital had happened.

Maverick had happened.

A low whuff and the *thunks* of a tail against hardwood floor drew her attention.

A group of five sled dogs that stole her heart also happened. None of these events were in the locums job description.

She held her hand out to Kenai for another doggy lick.

Lee stretched one more time, tensing from her toes all the way up to her head. She rolled over and hugged the pillow. She was so satisfied. So happy.

So torn.

She could see a future with Maverick. She trusted him to support her. She wanted to support him. It was true that she was falling in love with him.

Lee also needed to make a good decision for her own

future, which involved her financial security. Her future. She had always assumed she'd go back to northeast Georgia after she financially sorted out her life.

Hadn't planned on actually liking it here.

Actually liking someone here.

Then getting a better offer that would take pressure off her financial situation.

A better offer. She buried her face in the pillow.

Better for her heart or better for her life?

SHE COULD HEAR Maverick's low voice in the great room as he talked on the phone. She pulled her clothes on and quietly opened the bedroom door.

With his back to her, he wandered across the great room near the windows, gesturing with one hand. His untucked flannel shirt covered dark utility pants.

Before she could hear what he was saying, her phone that had been tossed on the bedside table rang. She dove for it, not wanting to disturb him or a snoring Kenai.

"Hello?"

"Dr. Tipton?" A woman's warm voice reached her.

"Yes."

"Hi, this is Kayla from TempHealth, hoping to touch base with you on my text and email regarding that Utah assignment. Did you get a chance to look things over?"

The pertinent parts, like how much she would make there. She glanced toward the door as a knot formed in her stomach. "I, um, need to give it a little more thought. Isn't that a mean thing to do to the folks here? Removing me from this assignment?"

"It's not ideal, but it happens on occasion."

"Couldn't I pick up the new job after finishing up here?"

"No, they're interviewing multiple candidates and will make a decision in the next week."

"Week?" Sweat cooled on her forehead. Her grip on the phone became slippery.

"This *is* one of the most lucrative contracts I've seen in my ten years of family medicine locums recruiting. Never say never, but I don't believe you'll see another offer close to this anytime soon."

Lee stalled by asking questions. "I'd still be doing the full scope family medicine and obstetrics I'm practicing now?"

"Yes. Including low-volume ER work."

"In a warmer climate closer to amenities like shopping?" Stupid question. Until she had a financial buffer, Lee was done shopping for anything other than groceries and necessary items.

"Yes. Much warmer than where you are."

"And they want to pay me double the amount?"

"Exactly."

Her body shook. How could she make this decision?

How could she not?

"More money? Are you sure?"

"Twice as much."

Damn it. She knew what the balance was in her bank account. She knew her debt load. She knew what double her

214

current income meant.

She also knew … other things that weren't financial.

"When do you need my answer?"

"By next Monday at the very latest. Sooner is better."

"All right, you'll have it by then." With shaking hands, she ended the call.

And looked toward the doorway.

Where a tall, handsome, unhappy Alaskan guy stood.

"How much did you hear?" she asked.

"Enough."

Chapter Twenty-Five

MAV'S EARS BUZZED.

She was leaving.

For money.

And *shopping*.

"So. Was *this* not to your liking?" He moved his hand in an arc to indicate that *this* meant Yukon Valley, the hospital, the babies, and him.

"It's not like that—"

"I know what I heard." When he swallowed, the action felt like sand and tasted like failure. "This isn't my first time with someone from the lower forty-eight thinking they want the Alaskan lifestyle. Until they hate it here."

"I don't hate it here."

"But it's not enough." *I'm not enough.* Just like before. "Damn it, you'd think I would have learned by now."

"This is a complicated situation." She sat cross-legged on the bed, somehow withdrawing further into herself.

He'd seen a similar posture with Skylar years ago. After falling for the act in the past, he wasn't sure if he bought it today.

"I have to think of my financial situation," she said.

"You don't like it here. Right? Too cold, too far away

from shopping?"

Lee jumped to her feet, but didn't meet his eyes. "You're taking my words out of context."

"Context seemed pretty clear from where I'm standing."

"Damn it, Maverick. This is compl—"

"If you say *complicated* again, I may say something I will regret." Was that low growl his? Damn. "I'm not fancy. I work hard. I don't do 'complicated.' I am straightforward with everything I do."

"I know—"

He lifted his hand to stop her useless words. "This stay in Yukon Valley and being here with me. You were killing time until the next best thing came along."

Her warm brown eyes shimmered, the image of her pain nearly breaking him. "It sounds worse when you say it that way."

"At least now you can say you got the full Alaska experience."

She flinched like he'd physically hit her. He'd gone too far. He wanted to take back the words, but pride stuck his tongue in place.

With a voice barely above a whisper and her posture ramrod straight, she said, "We did not have sex as part of my *Alaska experience*. I am not casual about relationships."

"Sure. You pick guys you can help. Like we're a case to diagnose and cure?"

She recoiled. "What?"

Damn it. What had he said? "Here you are, the hero. You took care of this case, Lee. Good job. I mean it. You were great with handling Randy and thank you again for throwing your weight around as a doctor." *Stop talking*, his brain begged his mouth. Didn't work. He plowed ahead.

"And hey, you got your reward." He motioned in the general vicinity of his dumb penis. "Now you can go where the grass is greener." He hadn't wanted to say any of that, but his past memories took over and shoved those damned words out of the damn hole in his face. He held up a hand, hauling in air like he had run a mile. "Lee, I'm sorry. That was out of line. I shouldn't have said that."

"But you did say it." Her shuddering breath nearly drove him to his knees. "You weren't totally wrong."

Shit. "Which part was right?"

A sad, gulping laugh bubbled up. She stood there, in leggings and a thermal top and those cute wool socks, looking fragile and cold, and for a moment all he wanted to do was be her shelter to warm her up and take away her pain.

"You're right," she said. "I like to fix things. I try to make whatever situation I'm in a success, until it isn't. I like to help others, sometimes to my detriment. I'm tempted by the greener grass because it helps me solve the financial mess I'm in. A mess that I'm partially responsible for because of my own decisions. All of that is true."

He felt the shudder of her indrawn breath from across the room. Raw, painful emotion was written across her pinched expression.

She continued. "The other part that was true? That's the part where you're wrong. I do like Yukon Valley. I love the people here and all their silly quirks. I love your babies who look like disasters, but they are the most loyal team of dogs I could imagine. I love this lodge and the beautiful land around it."

What else did she love? He leaned forward to catch her whisper.

"I thought I was starting to fall in love with you."

"You thought." Mav hadn't hesitated. She had.

He knew for sure that he was falling in love with her. Knew that he needed Lee in his life. Right before she stepped out of it.

"Now I don't know." She sniffled. "Because now it doesn't matter. I need to make a decision that impacts my whole life and well-being."

"That decision won't involve me. Or Yukon Valley."

"I don't know yet."

Chapter Twenty-Six

T HE NEXT MORNING sucked more than usual Mondays. The sleepless night had left grit behind in Lee's irritated eyes.

Lee was on call, so she started her day in med-surg and saw the admitted patients, trying to bury herself in the routine of listening, analyzing data, considering the diagnoses, and formulating the best plan. It was familiar work but work she apparently couldn't do to formulate the best plan for her own life.

While listening to a patient's lungs, Lee peeked at the stark white world swirling outside the window. At its core, patient care was familiar, but she was still in an unfamiliar place. That cold landscape was as far as a person could be from the deciduous tree-covered and grassy hills of Georgia.

Her existence here was completely disconnected from mimosas on verandahs, brunching at country clubs, pleasant small talk with people who ran local and state governments, and comparing spring fashions. Lee glanced down at her salt-rimed knockoff Gianni Bini boots and chuckled while her patient inhaled again. Despite Lee's best efforts to keep the new footwear pristine, she had failed.

Those boots had retained their core purpose but changed

their identity.

Could Lee do the same?

The uncertainty behind any choice gnawed at her.

She exited the room and headed down the hall.

Before she entered the next room, she took a fortifying breath. "Knock, knock," she said.

"About time you got to me, Doc." Bruce's voice rang out.

"Hey, I'm saving the best for last!"

"Fine. When can I go home? They won't salt any of my food here. I need some bacon. Those nurses keep ordering me around." He huffed, then whispered, "They keep measuring my urine."

Good ol' Bruce, completely missing the point of a low-salt diet and how adhering to it could keep his heart healthy. Also, missing the point of strictly measuring his intake and output. If he was this pleasant in professional interactions, she wondered how Aggie put up with him at home. He must have been a real bear since coming home from the hospital a few weeks ago.

"Hey, you were basically not alive the last time you were in this hospital. On this recent admission, you looked pretty rough as well. Be thankful that you're able to protest today."

"I'd be more thankful with bacon." He crossed his hair-covered and thick arms over the floral hospital gown.

At least he could complain without gasping for breath, which was a big improvement from his dyspnea during the congestive heart failure flare-up a few days ago, which Lee guessed might be connected to his love of bacon and salt.

Not to mention his use of diuretic pills when he felt like it. Lee sighed. She could only help him if it was on his terms.

After his heart attack in the ER last month, Bruce had a cardiac catheterization with three coronary blockages successfully stented in Fairbanks. He came home a week later and began the outpatient cardiac rehabilitation program. Luckily, Yukon Valley Hospital had a respiratory therapist trained for the task, so Bruce didn't have to travel the long distance to Fairbanks. Now he could grumble at a local person instead of a highfalutin' big city cardiac rehab nurse in Fairbanks.

Today's exam showed improvement with decreased congestion in his lungs and improved oxygenation. His heart rate was stable without murmurs. Thanks to IV diuretics and compression stockings—and a low-salt hospital diet—the swelling in his legs had decreased.

He pointed toward his feet. "I can barely get these on. When can I stop wearing these stupid socks?"

"How about never? Those stockings help keep you alive, Bruce."

"Some life if I can't get them on because they're so tight." He set his jaw. "How about I use them until next week?"

"How about we get you one size larger socks that are easier for you to put on at home? Once your swelling stabilizes you can then go back to this size. Or you can use elastic bandages if you'd prefer."

"Hmmph." He flicked at the tape over his IV site.

Lee logged into the bedside computer. She reviewed the

daily vitals, fluid balance, and labs. His renal function was hanging in there, despite having his kidneys wrung out with diuretic.

The fine balance—help the heart and dry out the kidneys, or water the kidneys and overload the heart. It was a seesaw that needed to stay perfectly balanced—a job made extra challenging when someone added bacon.

"Dr. Burmeister did a great job tuning you up the past few days."

His answer was in the form of a grunt.

She clicked a few more tabs and nodded, satisfied with the information.

"You still courting that ambulance driver?" he said.

She choked on spit and turned toward him. "Bruce. Come on, now. Let's be professional here."

"So that's a no." He stroked his scruffy gray beard. "You want to date Calvin?"

His son, Calvin, an ER physician from Seattle, had stayed with Bruce in the hospital and was now spending a few weeks in town. One of the nurses mentioned that Calvin might stay on at least short-term for ER shifts at the hospital. The more help the better. Guilt prickled at her neck. Help would be especially needed here if she ended her assignment early.

"I'm sure your son is very nice, but no thank you," she mumbled.

"Why aren't you seeing Maverick anymore? You two got along like gangbusters when you were taking care of me with my heart attack."

Slinging her stethoscope around her neck so hard the bell *thunked* against her sternum, she winced and said, "Bruce, you were unconscious the entire time we cared for you. How in the world would you have firsthand observations about anyone who saved your life?"

"Hmm."

"Bruce?"

The grizzled man tried to appear innocent and pitiful. It didn't work.

"Spill it." She glared at him.

"Cripes, you're scary." He raised his hands. "Tuli said you two were a good pair."

She blew some hair back off her face. "He wasn't there, either!" Her voice rose on every word.

His gaze darted all over the room. "Well, he must have heard it from one of the nurses!"

Probably Deirdre or Amberlyn or Clyde. They all conspired to set her up. Billy the receptionist probably had an extra hand in stirring the pot.

Lee didn't need help being set up.

She needed help making a massive decision about her life. Take a leap … somewhere. That first step was proving to be the stumbling block.

The locums recruiter had already texted this morning, gently asking if she had any questions about the assignment.

Regardless, Lee's inner conflict would not be subject to Bruce's prying. "Does everyone know everything about everybody in Yukon Valley?" she snipped.

His eyes went wide. Mouth opened, then closed. "I plead

the Fifth."

"*Hmmph.*"

"That's my line."

"Well, I'm stealing it."

"So ... home?"

She crossed her arms and stared him down. "Here's the deal, Bruce. You have to adhere to the low-salt diet and eat healthy. Help me help you stick around so you can pester Aggie." She waited for him to nod. "You have the ability to out-eat and out-salt any amount of medication I prescribe. I can only do so much. Understand?"

"Yes, Doctor." Did he bat his eyes under those bushy brows?

She didn't buy the meek act for a minute. Shoving a strand of hair back behind her ear, she said, "Why don't we see how you do at home for a few days, and I can check on you in the office later this week?"

"It's a deal."

"*Hmmph.*"

Chapter Twenty-Seven

FOR THE NEXT several days, Mav threw himself into work on the lodge and with EMS. He had an ambulance service to keep running, no money to do it or enough medics on staff. Ditto with the lodge, which was now getting more inquiries and reservations.

Thanks to a certain woman who didn't know if she was sticking around or not. Didn't know if she wanted to be in Yukon Valley or if she would rather make extra money.

Yes, she deserved to recover from the financial blow her ex had given her. Mav could appreciate the difficulty of that situation. She deserved to get back on her feet again. He couldn't blame someone for having those goals.

Except for the fact that doing so might not involve him.

He couldn't count the number of times he had started a text to her, then deleted the message. What he really wanted was to sit with Lee in a room, hash their situation out, make promises that he could now deliver on, take back some of the words he had said, and hold on to her with both arms.

Instead, he worked and took care of the babies. Despite his busy schedule, he got out before or after his shifts to take the dogs for daily exercise. Even in terrible weather, their lolling tongues and happy yaps brought him a little bit of peace every day.

Now that there was a good chance he wouldn't have to give them up, it made him work that much harder to turn the lodge business into a success.

The booking volumes slowed down, but they kept on coming. He had requests to use the property as a wedding venue, a family reunion, and for various retreats. Mav shook his head. Whatever Tuli had done with that word-of-mouth social media blast had worked. Not only did they have bookings for almost every day Dee and Mav could host, but the lodge now boasted great reviews. Folks from town who had never stayed there posted about how much they liked Mav and Dee and what a beautiful property they had. Previous customers updated their reviews or added new ones. The uplifting support kept him going almost as much as the full schedule.

With the deposits for future reservations secured, he and Dee scraped together December's past-due mortgage payment along with January's and February's payments, keeping their heads above water and the property out of foreclosure. Barring unforeseen disasters, they would make future monthly installments on time. For the first time in forever, Mav didn't want to hide his mail.

After Lee had left his house on Sunday afternoon, he had opened the drawer that was stuffed full of bills and correspondence. The USGS letter confirmed what Randy had said about the minerals on the property. It explained how the initial survey had been misfiled. It described the legal process if he wanted to excavate himself or if he wished to lease the rights. USGS outlined the tax implications if the mine started producing. Sounded like a ton of regulations and safety processes, regardless of whether they mined for gold or extracted the rare earth elements.

The BLM letter referenced Randy's inquiries into Mav's property. Randy was looking for other ways to access targeted points bordering the property. The guy wanted to mine the vein with or without owning Mav's land. Based on BLM's wording, their response to Randy's request for access to adjacent land wasn't just *no*, but *hell no*.

Early in the week, Mav had contacted Alaska Mining Claims to ensure the property was safe from any other outside speculation or prospecting. The discovery of ores and minerals in the area might benefit everyone in town, and Mav and Dee were discussing it with other citizens who might have involved property.

If his bed seemed empty, he was too busy to think about it, except late at night in the period of minutes between lying down and falling asleep.

Lee wasn't Skylar. Mav could see the vast differences in those situations now. He was a different man now, too.

He wanted to fight for Lee. Convince her of what was right in front of her.

She loved Alaska. He had seen it in her eyes. Heard it in the way she described the land around her and the people in this town.

The connection they had was real. Damn it, he deserved a chance to see where it could go. He wanted to be a support for her.

He wanted to be enough for her.

The choice was no longer his.

Lee would make a decision soon, if she hadn't done so already.

When Mav had questioned Dee, she hadn't heard anything definitive about Lee's plans.

He pressed his hand to the empty pillow next to him, imagining her tart and sweet salmonberry scent.

Today was Wednesday. He'd text her tomorrow. They needed to talk.

Chapter Twenty-Eight

E ARLY THURSDAY MORNING, Lee answered her phone on the third ring as she walked down the hall to the empty doctors' lounge. "Hi, Mom." It was eleven back home. This call was later than the usual morning verandah and social pages chat. Also unusual on a weekday, but sometimes Mom called when the spirit moved her.

"Hi, doodlebug. How are you?"

"Good. Been busy. Five inpatients and a delivery yester-day—"

"Uh-huh. That sounds nice. Done any shopping lately?"

"What? No." A few weeks ago, she had quit shopping online or in person for anything other than absolutely necessary supplies. She'd decided to let those credit cards recover and her bank account catch its breath.

"That's nice." Mom's sip came through the connection. Probably enjoying her usual mimosa. "So, a little over a month until you finish that job and you'll be home again. We can't wait."

"Mm."

"When you get back, your father and I have a dinner planned for you. We invited some friends over, including city council members. Dr. Lunsford from the Alpharetta family practice clinic will be there, too. You can talk with him about joining the group."

First of all, the attendees were her parents' friends. Not hers. This dinner had little to do with Lee and everything to do with small town political networking and keeping up appearances.

Secondly, Dr. Lunsford and his colleagues were all nice people. But compared to the broad scope of rural medicine she could practice, a suburban Atlanta outpatient clinic wasn't the kind of setting that best fit her skills and the parts of family medicine that were meaningful to her.

"No, Mom, that's not the plan—"

"Oh, and Preston can't wait to see you. I'm sure you and he will get right back together. He'll be at dinner. It'll be good for his career that the city council members see you after your mission trip to Alaska."

Lee sighed. "First of all, this is a job. I'm working for a rural hospital. It's not a mission trip. This isn't charity. Second of all, Preston and I are done, Mom. I'm sorry that you feel this is information you have to hide." She settled on the doctors' lounge couch. "I'm not sure why you are so invested in his career—he's not even your son. Regardless of the reason, you have to let it go. I have."

That was a true statement. She had cut the anchors weighing her down. She had committed to repairing her finances while also providing rural medical care.

She needed to contact the recruiter later today.

"I just thought ..." Mom trailed off.

Lee rubbed her forehead. In addition to the financial

issues, she had her personal baggage, but now she had tools to better evaluate her decisions, trust her own judgment—for her career and her relationships—and set boundaries.

Take this conversation, for example.

She ran a hand through her hair and leaned back. "Mom, I love you, but I need you to hear me. This is the last time I am going to say this. Preston and I are no longer together. We were well and truly divorced as of several months ago. We were separated long before that. He did bad things. He's not a good person. Do with that information as you and Dad see fit. I am not going to associate with him."

There was a sharp intake of air. "Seems selfish to me. What will people think? What am I supposed to tell the city council members?"

Ugh. Lee counted to ten.

Right around the number six, Mom delicately coughed and said, "Well, you'll see things differently when you are back home. Not sure how you stand it out there. I saw on The Weather Channel where there was a big blizzard in Anchorage. Hope you were okay."

Lee began counting again, then gave up. "I'm not sure I'll be coming back to Georgia. Not long-term. I enjoy the work I'm doing. I like being able to use all of my skills to make a meaningful impact on the local community. I don't mind the rural life. It's peaceful." Most of the time.

Mom gasped, and Lee visualized her clutching pearls.

She continued, "And I know it's hard to understand, but Alaska is huge. What you're describing is like saying a blizzard in Atlanta is going to affect people living in

Michigan."

A sniff. "Well, it would if it's a big enough storm."

Lee held her tongue. "Fair enough."

Silence spread out between them like an old lace tablecloth.

"Still there?" Lee asked.

"Yes."

"But?"

"Your father and I will miss you."

"Wherever I am, you can always come visit. I'll be back from time to time."

"Where would I stay?"

"Best cross that bridge when we get to it."

A clink of a glass on the verandah tabletop. "You're happy?"

She sat up straight. "Yes, I truly am. It's been a rough few years, and this work is good for me in so many ways." It was a relief to finally articulate her thoughts to Mom.

Another weight lifted from her shoulders.

"You have friends?"

"Oh my gosh, I'm thirty-five and you're asking about friends?" Lee chuckled. "Yes. Lots of friends, Mom."

"Then I'm happy for whatever it is you do out there."

Lee swiped at her damp cheek. "That means a lot."

Chapter Twenty-Nine

"SEE, WITH THIS whole Dr. Tipton situation, what you need to do is take that relationship bull by the horns, Mav." Tuli stood behind the deli counter on Friday evening and made a ridiculous horn-grabbing motion with his hands.

Louise smirked and drank her Three Bears coffee. Their EMS shift had started an hour ago. No calls so far, which meant Mav and his partner could grab a snack before the store closed.

Unfortunately, no calls meant that Tuli, the area fire chief, remained at his post at the Three Bears deli, with an abundance of free time and opinions.

Tuli's gregariousness had reached a whole new level of annoying tonight.

Mav's mood? Not quite as good. He had texted Lee about getting together to talk, and she seemed to push it off until later this weekend. Since receiving her reply, a knot of dread had lodged in his gut.

Yesterday, Dee and the CEO had made an official offer from the hospital for Lee's permanent employment here in Yukon Valley. Technically, it was a counteroffer to the proposed Utah locums gig. Unfortunately, Yukon Valley, while in need of good doctors, wasn't flush with money. The way his sister explained it, the offer was heartfelt but not lucrative.

To his knowledge, Lee hadn't signed anything yet. No word.

Which meant, no word on Mav and Lee's future. He had given her space. Now he wanted to clear the air and make his own offer.

Mav smirked at Tuli's antics. "What would you know about taking the relationship bull by the horns?"

His friend's gaze flicked toward Louise and away, but not before a crimson flush crept up his neck. Huh, so it was like that, was it?

Tuli opened and closed his mouth.

Mav shrugged. "All I'm saying is, sometimes it's better to give people the time they need, and—" His phone alarmed. Dispatch.

Louise silenced her phone that rang at the same time. Digging in her EMS coat pocket, she fished out the keys to the rig and silently raised her eyebrows at Tuli as they exited. In the passenger seat, Mav punched in the address while Louise pulled out of the parking lot and flipped on the flashing lightbar on top of the rig.

The location seemed familiar. Male, age sixty-eight, respiratory distress.

The address clicked. "Ah crap, it's Bruce."

"Not again." Louise maneuvered out of town for several miles, then down the secondary gravel road. The snow still held up as a decent road base this first week in February, but in another month, they'd be fighting gray silty mud and massive potholes as an entire season of snow melted into one big sloppy mess.

In a flash, they arrived at Bruce and Aggie's place. Aggie met them at the door and ushered them into the cozy cabin where Bruce sat in his recliner. He looked … stable. Comfortable. The house smelled of fresh baked goods.

"How's it going?" Mav asked him.

"Little short of breath, little chest pain." He scowled at Aggie. "The usual."

Louise got a set of vitals while Mav listened to his heart and lungs. "Sounds okay."

Bruce glared at the inflating blood pressure cuff. "And chest pain," he reminded them, patting his chest.

Louise shrugged along with Mav and hooked up the oxygen tank. Given the health scare that Bruce had gone through last month, if the man felt he needed to be in the ED, no one would argue.

"Let's get the gurney," Mav said.

"Naw, I can walk." Bruce tried to get out of the chair.

He made a swiping motion with his hand. "Rules are rules."

"That's not what I wanted. I just need to get to the hospital so that—" He clamped his mouth shut.

"So that what?" Mav said.

Aggie tapped Bruce on the shoulder. "So that he can make sure everything is going to be okay."

"*Hmmph.*"

She pinned him with a terrifying glower. "Go with them." Aggie patted her gray curls. "I will be along shortly.

Might bring cookies for everyone. You all work so hard at the hospital."

"Ooh, chocolate chip?" Louise asked as she reentered the house and locked the brakes on the stretcher.

"Would you like one now?"

"Yes, ma'am. Thank you." She removed her exam gloves, applied hand sanitizer, then took a cookie off the plate Aggie brought over and chewed in happiness.

Mav didn't want to be rude. After cleaning his hands, he selected one as well. The chocolate was melted, so he ate it quickly.

From the recliner seat, Bruce waved his hands. "Hello? I could be having a heart attack, people. Let's go."

"Are you sure you're feeling okay, Bruce?" Mav said. "At what point in your life have you ever willingly sought medical care?"

"Uh, today's different." He pressed on his sternum.

"Okay, okay. Let's get you down the road." Mav pulled on a fresh pair of gloves and motioned for Louise to position Bruce so they could move him safely. "Say, where's Calvin? You literally have an ER doctor staying with you."

Aggie frowned. "He ran over to Fairbanks this weekend for supplies."

They quickly secured Bruce to the gurney, with monitors and oxygen all attached, and wheeled him out to the ambulance. Within minutes, they arrived at the ED ambulance entrance and rolled him down the hall.

"Which room?" Mav asked.

Amberlyn pointed at trauma bay two.

"Hey, Dee, working late tonight?" Mav waved at his sister, who walked into the department.

She didn't meet his eyes. "Yep."

As soon as they transferred Bruce to the hospital bed, he looked at Mav, Louise, and Amberlyn and hollered, "I want the doctor. I don't feel good."

Amberlyn's eyes widened, and she shot out of the room. "Be right back."

Wait. Wasn't the nurse supposed to stay with her patient? Mav shook his head at Louise as he quickly transferred the pulse-ox and telemetry leads to the ED machines. Out in the hallway, the buzz of voices rose and fell.

He distinctly heard someone say, "Oh, cookies." Aggie must have arrived.

A rap of knuckles against metal doorframe preceded a familiar voice. "Knock, knock, Bruce. What's going on today?"

Lee skidded to a stop a few feet into the room, looked at Mav, and gave him a shy smile.

His heart flopped in his chest. Honest-to-God flopped. "Hi."

"Hi, yourself. How are you?"

"Not bad. On shift tonight."

"Um, I can see that." She pursed her lips. "You doing okay?"

"Good. Real good."

Louise coughed the word *awkward* and smirked before turning back to work on Bruce.

Suddenly, Lee reached out. "Bruce, stop! What are you

doing? Get back up there."

As Louise unattached the last EKG lead from Bruce, he high-fived Louise and they traded matching grins.

Mav's brain had trouble keeping up.

"Took you two long enough. Now sort things out already. I went to a lot of trouble and lost more chest hair with those stupid sticky electrode things. Almost had to get in one of those air-conditioned gowns again," Bruce said, tromping past and pulling the room curtain behind him. "What took you people so long? Aggie! I'd like my cookie now, dear."

Louise slipped out as well, sliding the glass trauma bay door closed.

"Wait. What just happened?" Lee tilted her head, brow furrowed.

"It's not April Fool's Day," Mav said once he closed his mouth.

That was when it hit him. They'd been set up by Bruce, Aggie, Louise, Dee, and the Yukon Valley ED night shift.

Chapter Thirty

LEE DIDN'T MOVE for a full minute.

She had been meaning to talk with Maverick this week, but work had gotten in the way. Truth be told, she'd avoided him. Calling the locums recruiter earlier today had been difficult enough.

Big decisions took time. Big decisions came with risk.

"Hi," he said.

"You already said that."

"Wasn't sure how else to start again." He shrugged off his beanie and coat and rested them on the bed. She resisted the urge to smooth his unruly hair.

Lee bit her lip. "How about we park ourselves on the edge of this barely used hospital bed and chat."

His quick smile eased her tension. "Works for me." After they both sat, he said, "How are things?"

"Good. Better." She paused. "How's the business?"

"Great. Dee and I have our schedules full with guests." Even though he smiled, tense lines bracketed his eyes and mouth. He was still handsome with his tousled hair and his broad shoulders. "This week was busy with the dogs, working on the business, and EMS—those are like three full-time jobs," he added.

A flash of concern hit her as she read the fatigue on his face. "You're taking time to rest?"

"You know how it goes. Unpredictable schedules are part of the territory."

Couldn't argue that fact. "How are the babies?" It had only been a handful of days, but already she missed Kenai's trusting brown eyes and Bob's goofy overbite.

His blue gaze locked on to her. "They miss you." Mav's low voice wrapped around her like a warm embrace.

"Just the dogs?"

"No. Not just the dogs." He started to say more, then stopped.

"I ..." She cleared her throat and started again. "This week has been hard, figuring things out."

"Same here."

She froze. "Oh?"

"Normally, I'm all about ladies first, but I need to say some things to you."

Being the focus of his blue eyes scared her. She'd never seen him this serious.

Given everything, he had every right to speak his piece first. "Okay."

He stiffly perched on the edge of the bed, his face cut from stone. "What happened last weekend was a mistake."

"Oh. Boy." She sucked in a harsh breath and blinked hard against burning eyes. Gripping the edge of the mattress, she braced for what was about to happen.

"Wait. Damn it, that came out wrong," he said. "What I mean is I made a mistake in what I said to you. I said that I was just a case for you to diagnose and fix. That you were here to get the Alaska experience and then you'd leave." A muscle jumped in his jaw. "I cut both of us off at the knees with those words, and that was wrong. I made assumptions and dumped some of my own baggage on your shoulders, and that was wrong."

"I do try to help folks. Maybe too much, as it turns out." She gestured, and he caught her hand with his, holding her lightly so that she could easily pull away if she wanted to.

"If you mean with your ex, he's an idiot. No offense." He rubbed his thumb over the back of her hand, the action familiar and comforting. "You're amazing at helping others. I can't tell you how much I appreciated how you stuck your neck out for me and my sister last weekend." His voice dropped. "I love how you and I work so well together, professionally and otherwise. I love our connection. I want more." He paused and pressed his mouth into a tight line.

"But?" Oh, this was going to hurt.

"Deep down, I presumed you'd be like other people who weren't from the area and, like those people, eventually you'd hate it here and leave. Then, when I overheard your conversation with the locums person, I jumped to the conclusion that everything I had assumed had come true."

"It's not like that."

He gently squeezed her hand. "I know. It wasn't fair for me to judge you based on my history. It wasn't fair for me to judge your situation and decisions, based on me." He flashed a grin. "Not that I wouldn't love for you to base your decisions on me."

Sweat prickled at her lower back. "To be fair, I did make a decision this week, and it only partially involved you. The rest of the decision? I had to do what was right for myself." She swallowed around a lump in her throat. "I was going to talk with you tomorrow, but I probably would have chickened out."

"This is going to suck, isn't it?"

"Depends."

"Damn."

"I enjoy my practice here in Yukon Valley. It's a nice group of people. I like working with everyone."

"But."

"I'm scared."

He shifted to face her more squarely, but said nothing. Instead, he simply sat and listened.

"It's different here. I don't know for certain that this will be a fit. I mean, it's beautiful here. I like the people. I feel more like myself in this place than I did in Georgia."

"Still hearing the *but*." His warm voice wrapped around her like a hug.

"I need to stand on my own two feet financially. Be a confident, complete person first before getting into a long-term relationship. I need to trust myself to choose someone that won't hurt me." *Damn it.* She swiped at a tear. "Sorry. This is heavy stuff."

"I'm glad you trust me with this." Maverick tucked a piece of hair behind her ear. "What do you need from me?"

"Oh my gosh, you're wonderful," she gushed. "This, right here. The support and patience. Problem is, I don't know long it will take me to trust myself or the situation. I don't know when I'm going to feel financially safe with a partner again."

"The last thing I want is for you to feel like you rushed to make any decision. But let me say this. I am falling in love with you. I want to try and make something work between us. Yes, I want you," he leaned forward and whispered. "Naked on this hospital bed, if I could get away with it."

Her shudder turned into a laugh. "Guessing the credentialing organizations would not look kindly on that sort of bed utilization."

"Customer satisfaction would be high."

"True."

"What I need you to hear is that you're worth waiting for. If you want to try for a relationship, then I'm willing to be as patient and creative as needed."

"Wow, Maverick. That's—no one has ever said anything like that."

"Now, see, that's a crime." He drew her hand up and brushed his lips over the palm.

Pulling in a big breath, she said, "I turned down the Utah job. I'm going to finish out the assignment here through March, then move to a permanent position in Yukon Valley."

"That's great news!"

"I'm a little scared from a financial point of view. But I need to trust myself to be responsible and to trust my instincts about the people around me."

"If ever I make you feel uncomfortable—financially or

otherwise—you have to let me know."

"It's mostly a matter of depending on my own gut again." She pulled his hand to her so she could rest her cheek against it. "You, I can depend on." She glanced up.

He watched her, steady, waiting.

God, she didn't deserve this level of patience. "If you're willing to give this … us … a go, then I'm in a good place to try."

With a sharp shake of his head, he said, "I don't want to try."

Disappointment dropped like a brick into her stomach. "Oh. I mean, sure. Okay. That's for you to decide, and I understand."

"Lee." He let go and cupped her jaw with both of his hands.

"Yes?"

"I'm not interested in a half-assed relationship with you. Not maybe. Not try. I need to know we're both working toward something meaningful."

Her heart thumped as she nodded. "I want you, Maverick. I want the guy who loves his dogs and rescues people from car accidents. I want the man who enjoys minus-twenty-degree weather and who values me for who I am."

"Lee, you have no idea how much you mean to me. You're an amazing woman and I need you in my life."

"So that means …"

"Um."

"That we're …"

Lines formed around his eyes as he gave a sheepish grin.

"I believe the phrase is *it's complicated.*"

She snorted. "It fits."

He leaned over and brushed a kiss over her temple, drawing out shivers. "Wait. Are we allowed to kiss if it's complicated?"

"Hope so." She lifted her face to him as his mouth swept against hers, again and again, until she could taste his lips and smell his fresh air and spruce scent deep in her soul.

Outside the trauma bay doors, faint cheers filtered back to them.

Maverick froze, his hand still on her jaw with fingers splayed into her hair. His lips were an inch away.

A light growl came from his throat. "I'm going to kill all of them."

Then as one, Lee and Maverick stood, ducked around the privacy curtain, and peered through the glass.

Everyone—Dee, Louise, Amberlyn, Clyde, assorted other staff, Bruce and Aggie—crowded around the ED security monitor screen off to the side of the work area.

Lee looked up at the fisheye in the exam room and waved. "Are you kidding me? Okay, y'all, yes, you can see us. Is there no privacy in this place?"

Maverick laced his fingers in hers as he pulled her in for a warm hug. Then they opened the trauma bay door and everyone rushed over to them.

"So? How'd it go?" Dee said. "We had visual but no sound."

Warmth rose over Lee's neck. "That's a privacy violation!"

"It is a public place of business," Dee said, crossing her arms. "It's not *our* fault you used it for a private conversation. Also, you're not patients." She paused. "Don't worry. I turned off the sound. You're welcome."

Maverick tapped their joined hands against his leg and grinned down at Lee. "You're the HIPAA expert."

"She's right," Lee huffed. "We can't sue."

Bruce picked up another cookie from the plate on the counter but dropped it when Aggie lightly smacked the back of his hand. "Can I go back home now? I want to watch my program."

"That was an expensive way to pull one over on us, Bruce," Maverick said.

"Eh, worth it." He nodded to Lee. "Well?"

She smiled up at Maverick, who lifted his chin. "I'm staying on in Yukon Valley, and we're, uh, now both, um … It's complicated," she managed.

"Taking things slowly!" Maverick wrapped her up in another big hug, then got pulled away as everyone took turns congratulating both of them.

In the middle of the chaos and happy chatter, the EMS phones went off on Maverick's and Louise's hips.

"Gotta go," he said, giving Lee a quick kiss and running back to snag his hat and coat from the trauma room.

"I'll be here." Lee pulled his palm to her cheek, then shooed them out the door.

Another call night and another adventure in Yukon Valley.

The End

Acknowledgments

As always, big thanks to agent Jana Hanson who has believed in this book from the very beginning.

Thank you as well to editor Julie Sturgeon. I repeat this same phrase for every book she edits, but it holds true: Julie takes whatever I'm writing and makes it so much better. She's fabulous and patient, and I'm so grateful that my second act in publishing involves working with her again.

My appreciation also goes to medical romance writer Susan Carlisle, who provided me with support, encouragement, opportunities, and a much-needed beta read of the first portion of this book.

Hugs and a massive thanks to my readers. You have been so enthusiastic about this book, and your positive comments kept me writing! If there are folks who haven't signed up for my newsletter, where we basically chat about everything books and life and medicine, you can do so here: https://www.jilliandavid.net/newsletter-signup.html.

Thank you to all of the rural physicians, nurses, and staff members I've worked with over the past twenty years. Together we've laughed, cried, pranked each other, celebrated wins, and shook in our surgical booties. There never was enough time or personnel to cover all of the bases, but in the end, we cobbled together some amazing patient care in dicey situations and made a difference in people's lives.

To my patients, thank you for letting me be a part of your journeys. Whether we brought new life into the world, worked our way through a scary health crisis, or gathered around a bed while a loved one passed away, I have been honored beyond words to be a part of those moments.

Author Notes

Life imitates art in the strangest of ways. I've been a rural physician for my entire career. But when I wrote this book in 2021, I had never in a million years considered working as a locums physician! Fast forward to 2024 and I have several Ob or FP/Ob locums assignments under my belt, all in Absolutely Nowhere, USA. Thankfully, my book research corresponded with these real-life experiences! Phew.

I have so many comments about what is based on actual rural medicine in this book and what is embellished. Instead of listing all of that here, I encourage you to scoot over to my blog and check out some of the latest posts about Yukon Valley! Get all of the insider scoop here: https://www.jillian david.net.

About the Author

Award-winning and bestselling author Jillian David quickly writes then slowly edits medical romance, paranormal romance, and romantic suspense books. She loves to use medical situations and characters to drive drama in her books. Her favorite cell is the platelet and her least-favorite organ is the pancreas. She fully believes that curse words, when appropriately deployed during surgery, are hemostatic. Which also explains why no book of hers will ever bleed out…

Thank you for reading

Dr. Alaska

If you enjoyed this book, you can find more from all our great authors at TulePublishing.com, or from your favorite online retailer.

TULE
PUBLISHING

Made in United States
Troutdale, OR
04/03/2025

30308533R00146